Mastering Anime Drawing: Including Anime Anatomy, Eyes, and Hair

Step by Step Instructions on How to Draw 20 Anime

J.P. Manning

HOW TO DRAW ANIME - VOLUME 2

Introduction

Drawing stimulates parts of the brain that are responsible for creative thinking and imagination. From a young age, we are all creatively encouraged to draw, often to improve our fine motor skills and co-ordination.

From toddler 'scribbles' to 'matchstick men' you may find that as you get older you will want to tackle more complex drawings (perhaps it's an image you have seen in a book) but as you begin to put pencil to paper you may have no idea where to start, causing you frustration and annoyance.

With the help of our 'How to Draw' book series, this frustration will disappear as we guide you step by step, line by line, to create your very own masterpieces!

Each illustration in this book is deconstructed and simplified into lines and shapes that will not overwhelm you. As we guide you to form each simple line and shape together on the paper, the image gradually becomes more detailed and textured.

There will be such a sense of accomplishment and achievement once your drawing is complete, which in turn will boost your self-esteem and confidence.

Drawing Characters Step-by-Step

For the rest of the book I will show you how to draw 20 different characters step by step. Each step will build on the previous step until eventually you have 20 complete characters. The illustrations that I detailed on the previous pages will be included within these characters so please look out for them.

If at first, you find my step-by-step approach too complicated or difficult please leave it to one side and come back to it later. Instead, use the grids with numbers and letters on it first. By following the coordinates and matching them up with the coordinates on a blank grid you can redraw the characters that way instead.

What to do if you get frustrated whilst drawing

You may find that whilst working through my 'How to Draw' series, you may become frustrated as you find learning the new skill harder than you may have first anticipated. What you have drawn on the paper may be different to how you envisioned it to look, or you may be constantly comparing your skill to friends and siblings efforts. Learning a brand new skill can be difficult and time consuming, and you will need to remind yourself that everyone learns and works at different paces and that it is perfectly fine for you to take your time in refining your new skill.

If you find that your concentration is lost and you become agitated and frustrated with your work, it is very important to try and keep the activity fun and engaging, so encouraging regular breaks is imperative. It may even be better to encourage yourself to do a completely different activity for a while and come back to drawing tomorrow.

Validating your feelings is also crucial. It is okay for you to feel annoyed and frustrated, but always encourage yourself to keep trying. Perhaps tell yourself to take a step back in the book and repeat a part that they you have already mastered, then gradually move onto the step that you are finding trickier.

Everyone, including adults and the most successful artists can make mistakes, and sometimes these mistakes could even be successes! The extra line or shape you may have drawn accidently, could become part of the drawing as a whole and copying the lines exactly as they are in the book isn't a necessity.

However, drawing in pencil, rather than permanent ink, allows any 'mistakes' to be erased and learnt from. Being able to remove what you feel is a mistake will stop you from feeling overwhelmed and that you must start over from the beginning; instead you can carry on from the point you were able to erase out.

Try to always reinforce to yourself that the best way to learn when drawing is to learn from mistakes and continue on.

J.P. Manning

HOW TO DRAW ANIME - VOL 2

Here are all of the characters in this book. I guess it must seem like there is a lot of them when they are looked at all at once!

Luckily, I am not going to ask you to draw them all straight away. The best way to learn to draw is one step at a time. Each character in this book may require between 50 and 100 strokes of your pencil, but all you will need to think about is drawing one stroke at a time.

As you use your pencil, stroke by stroke, working your way through this book, you will eventually be able to draw all of the characters!

Welcome to How to Draw Anime

As you have been given this book, I am guessing that you love anime, and would like to learn how to draw them? Luckily, being interested is the most important thing of all in learning something new. To do your best, you must take your time, be patient and keep practicing.

How to draw anime eyes

I think a good place to start will be to learn how to draw anime eyes. Eyes come in all shapes and sizes, however in most cases anime eyes are on the larger side. Large eyes are suggestive of innocence and child-like characteristics.

Let us take a look at some different types of eyes

Drawing anime eyes step-by-step

Changing the size of your character's eyes in proportion to the size of the characters face can produce some interesting effects.

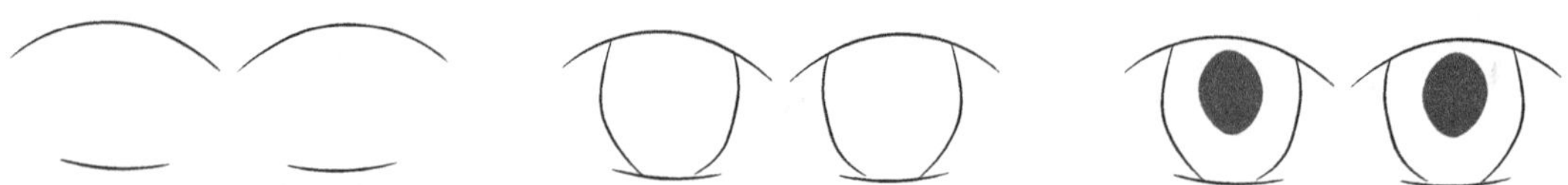

Here is an example of a character with different sized eyes

Here are some examples of anime hair

Sharp edges are a common theme.

Drawing anime hair step-by-step

Sometimes, if your character's hair is drawn first, it is quite easy to draw in a face afterwards.

Drawing anime facial outlines

Most anime facial outlines are oval with a sharp pointed chin. As a result, they can be drawn very quickly if needed. This can make it easier to draw cartoon strips quickly.

Anime noses

Anime noses are frequently minimalist and are often represented by a dot or a small curved line. This means that they can be drawn very quickly.

Drawing anime mouths

As with amine noses, anime mouths are frequently minimalist.
Different emotions can be displayed quite easily with very small
adjustments to a drawing.

Drawing Characters Step-by-Step

Now I have shown you the basics, if you follow the rest of this book
I will show you how to draw 20 different characters step by step.
Each step will build on the previous one until eventually you have
20 complete characters.

The illustrations that I detailed in the previous pages will be
included within these characters so please look out for them.

At first, you find my step-by-step approach too complicated or
difficult please leave it to one side and come back to it later. Instead,
you may want to use an alternative grid with numbers and letters on
it first. By following the coordinates and matching them up with the
coordinates on a blank grid you can redraw the characters this way
instead.

You can of course ask an adult to help you draw the grids instead, or
you may even feel able to draw them yourself.

1. Drawing a basic grid outline will help you to give your picture good proportions.

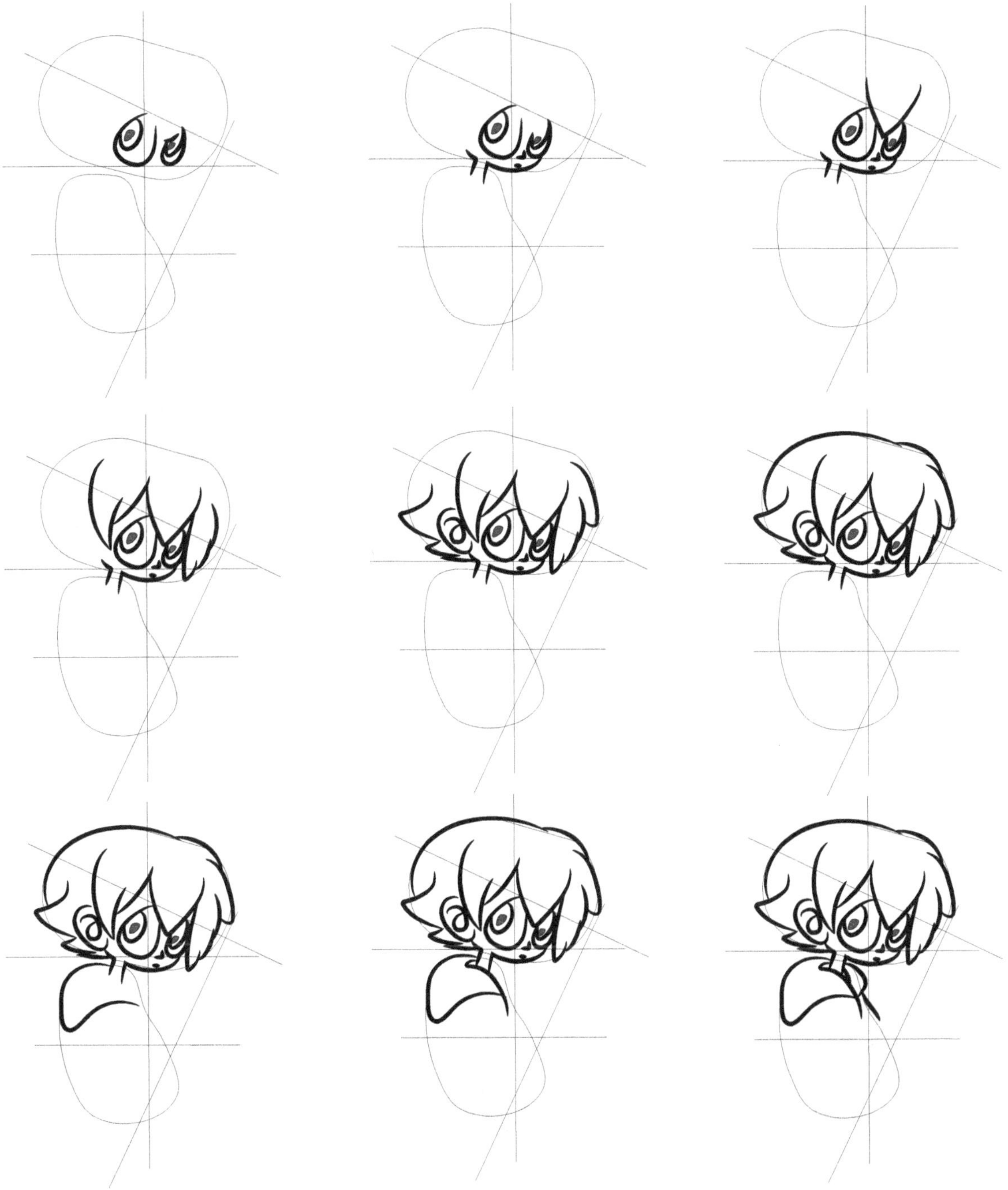

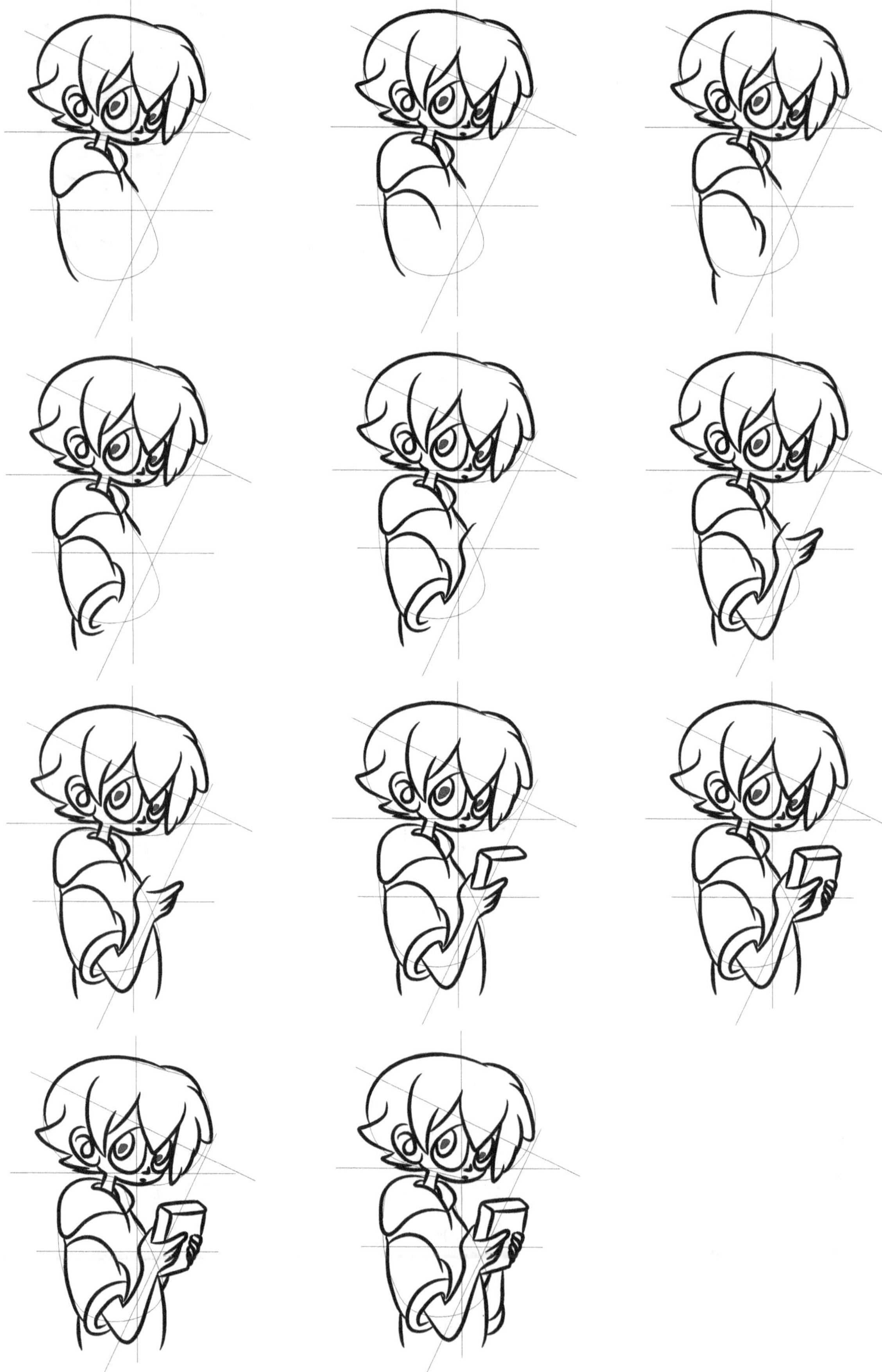

2. Building a basic stick character can often be
a useful way to get yourself started.

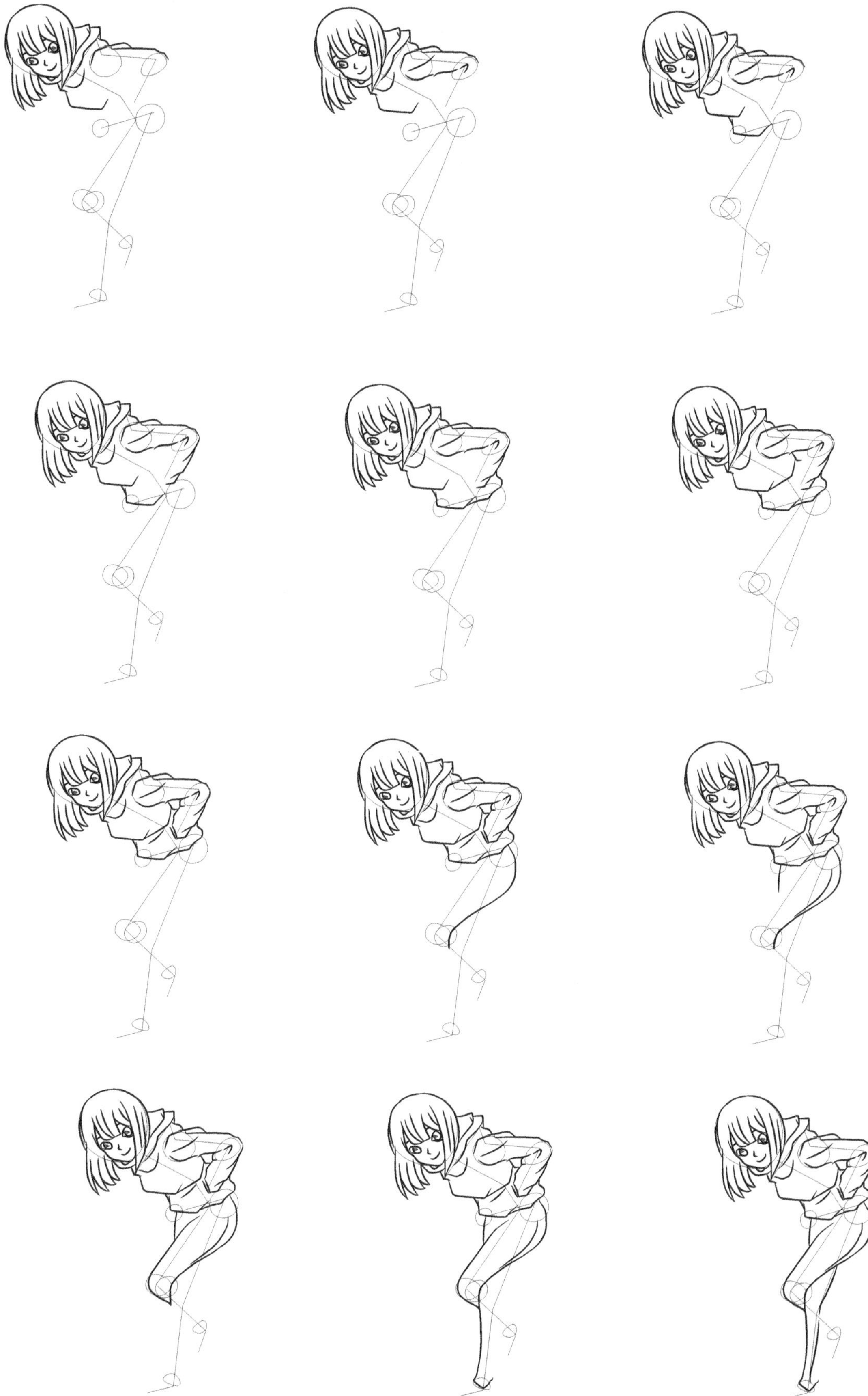

3. You can build your character around rough
outlines created in your grid.

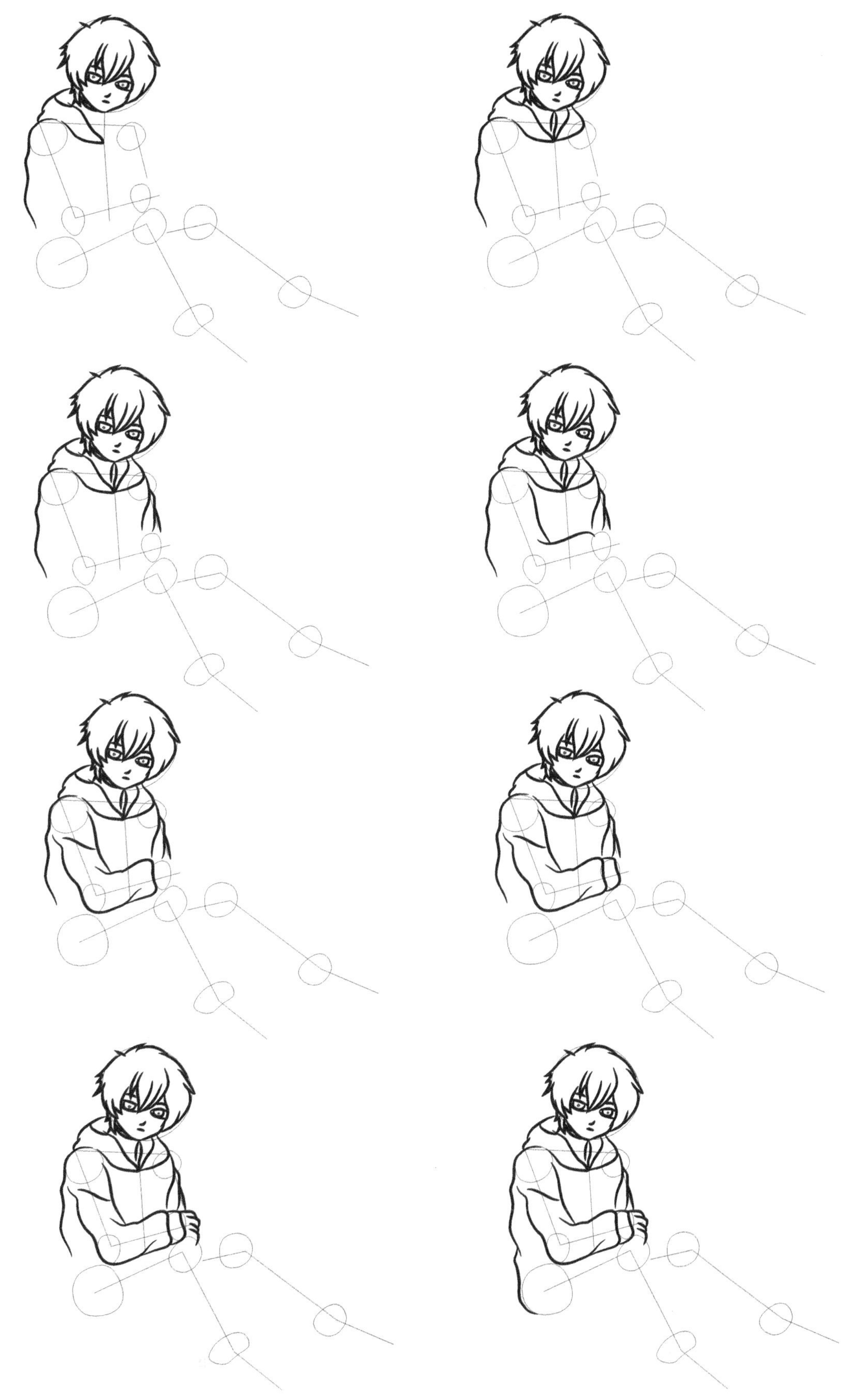

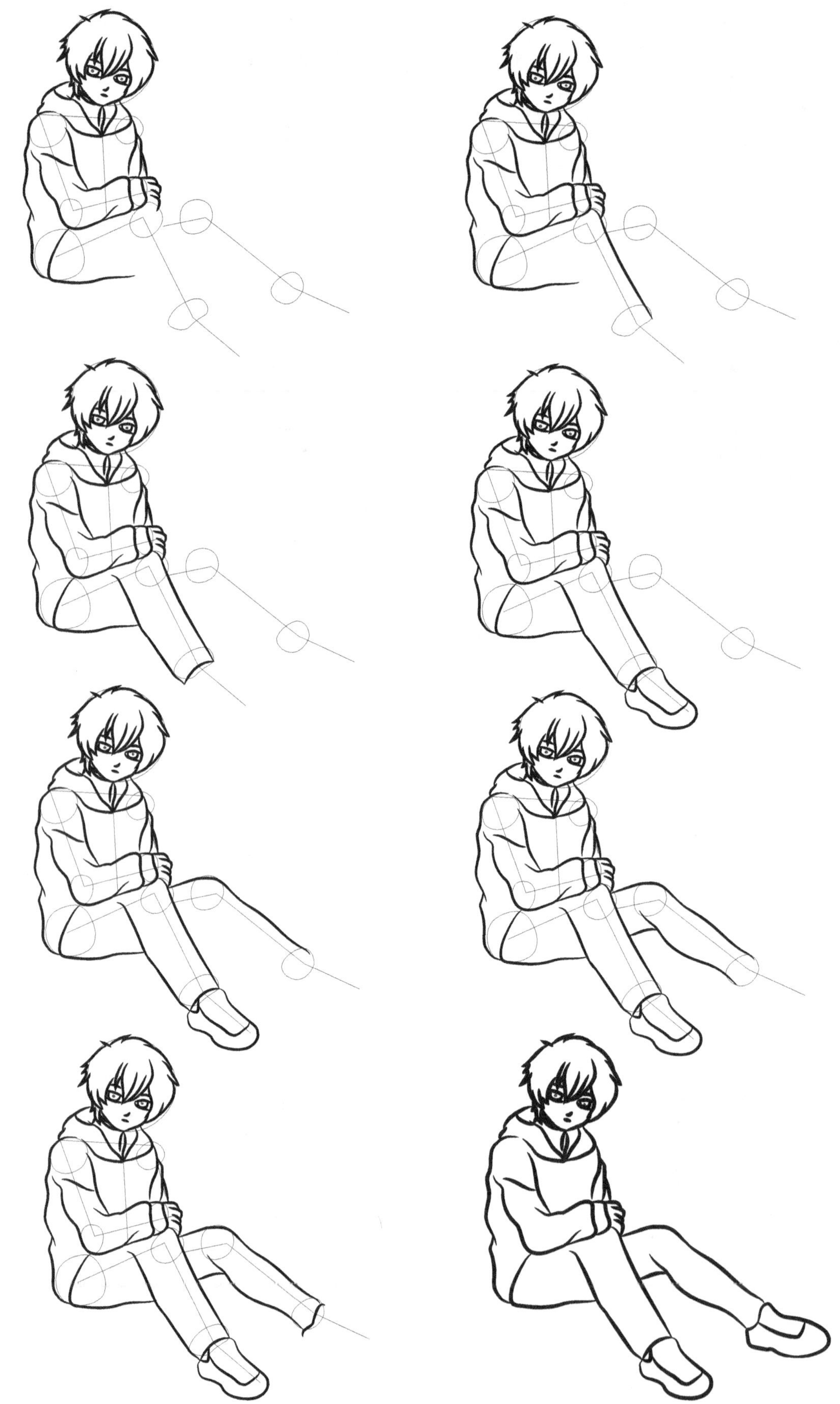

A B C D E F G H
1
2
3
4
5
6
7
8
9
10
11
12

4. The more information you can fit on your initial grid, the easier it will be to structure your drawing.

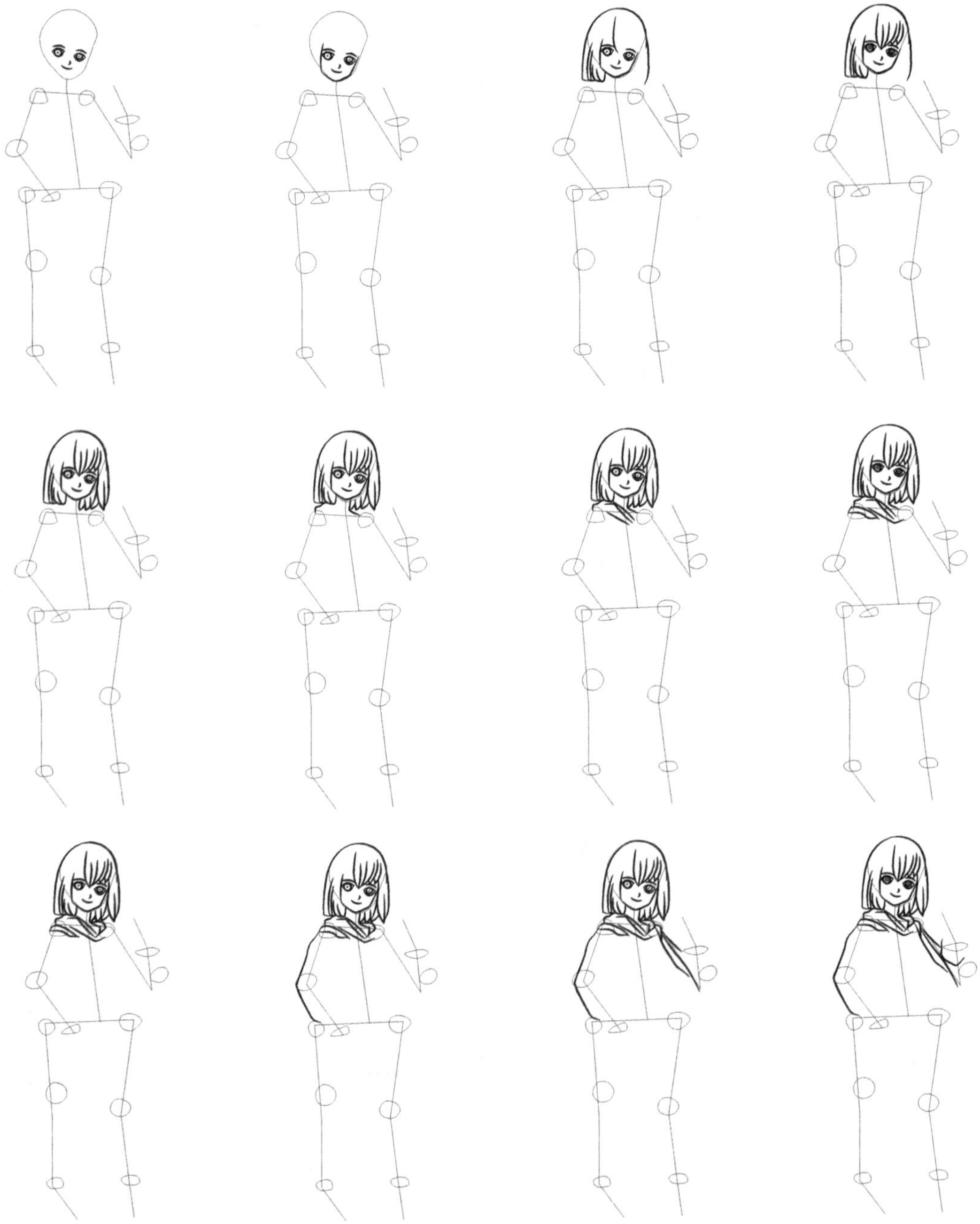

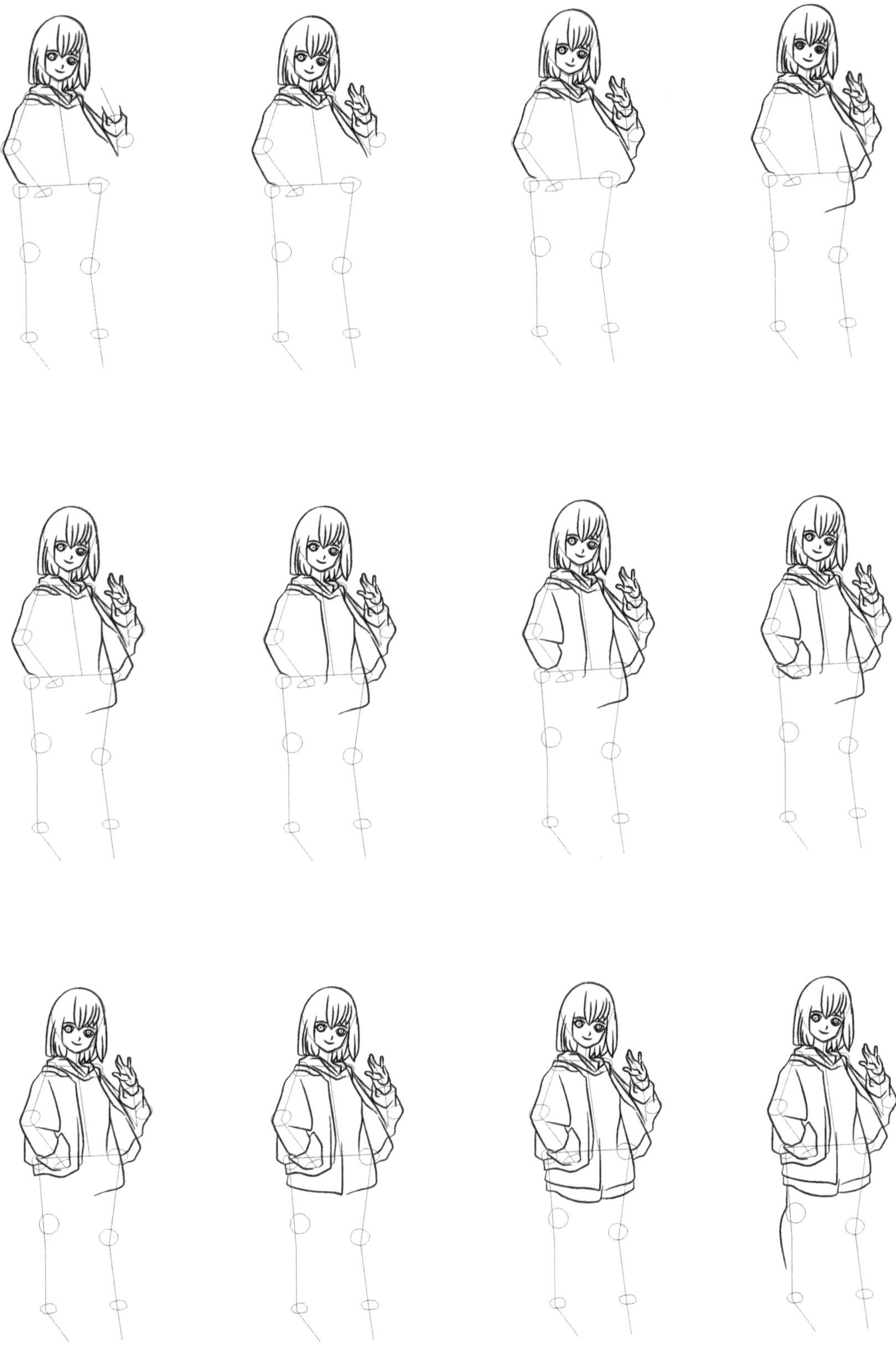

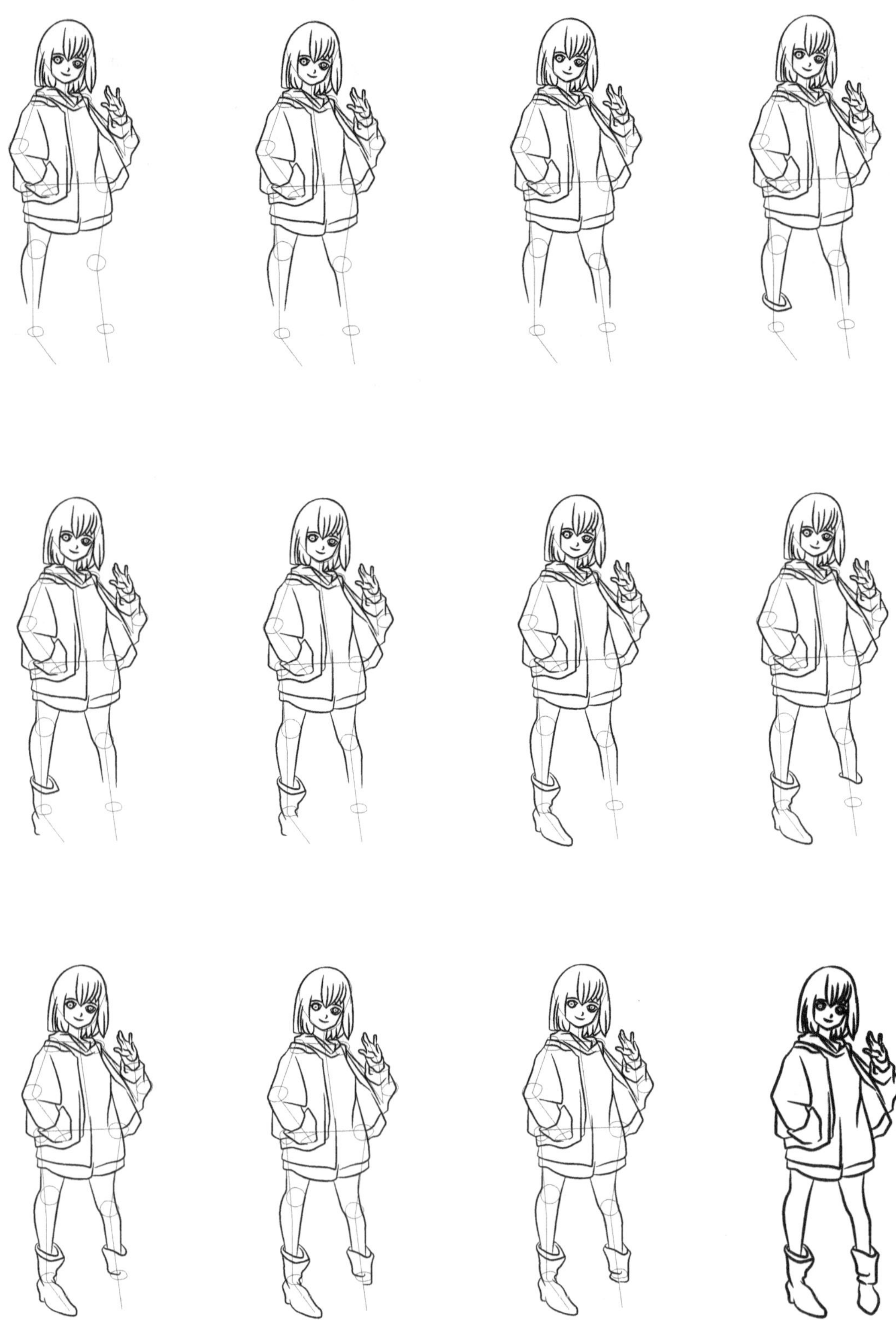

A B C D E F G H
1
2
3
4
5
6
7
8
9
10
11
12

5. Drawing is a process of construction. Add
one small part at a time.

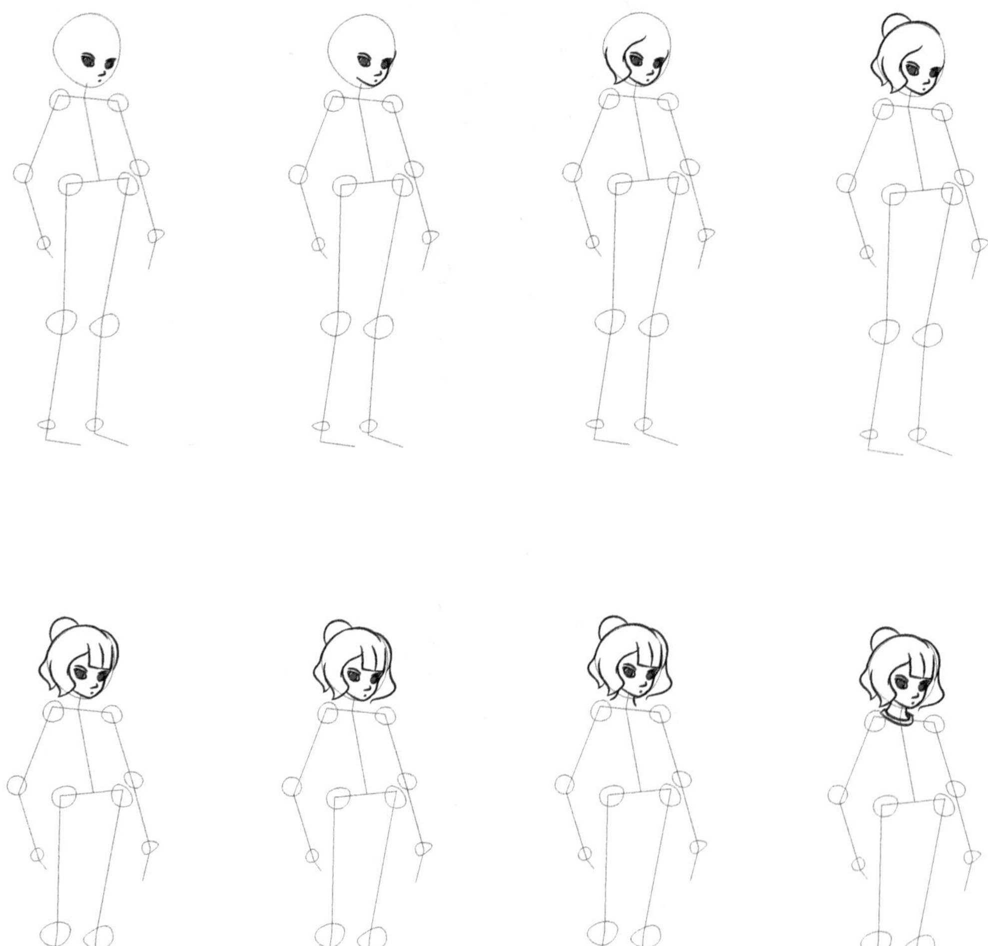

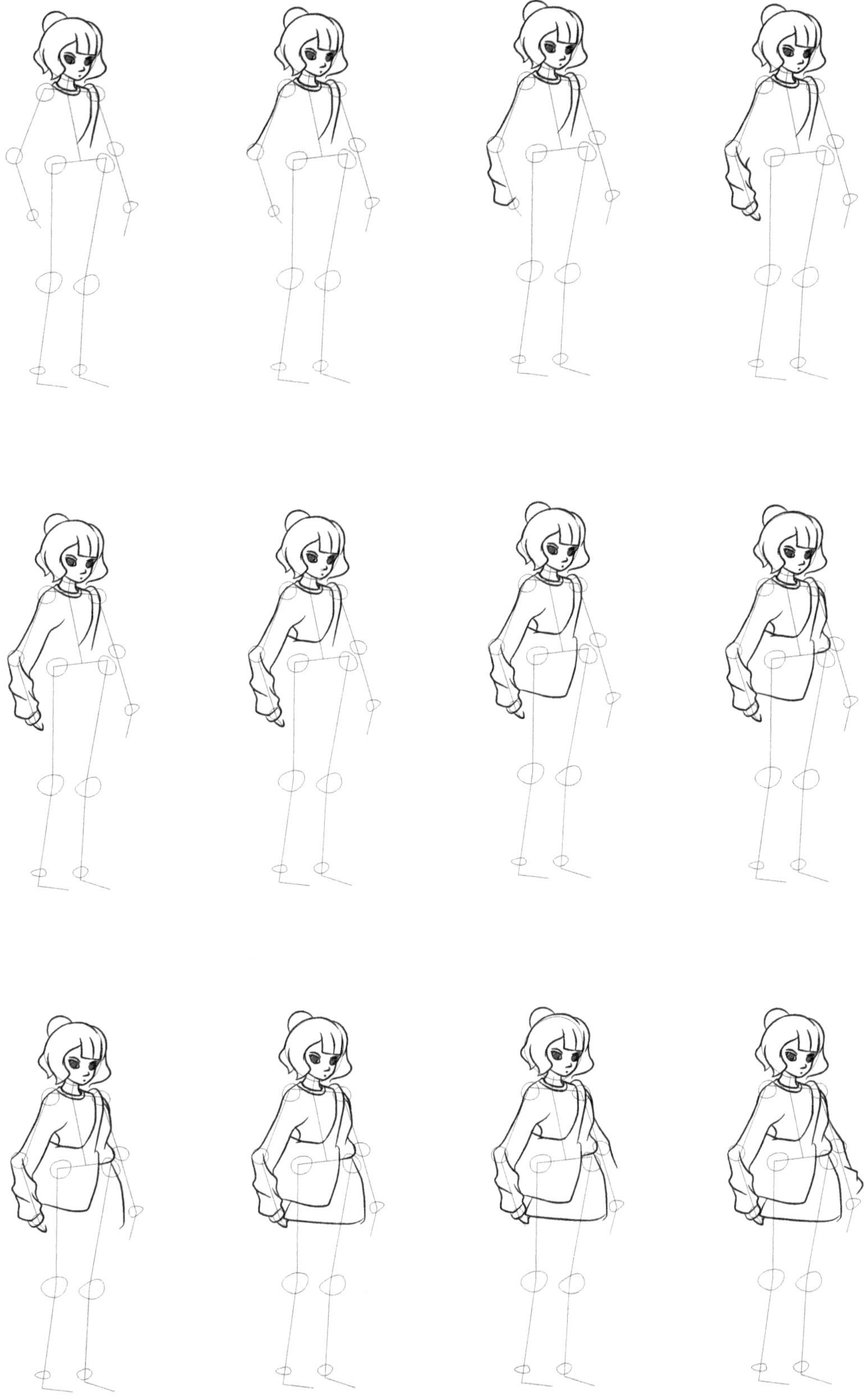

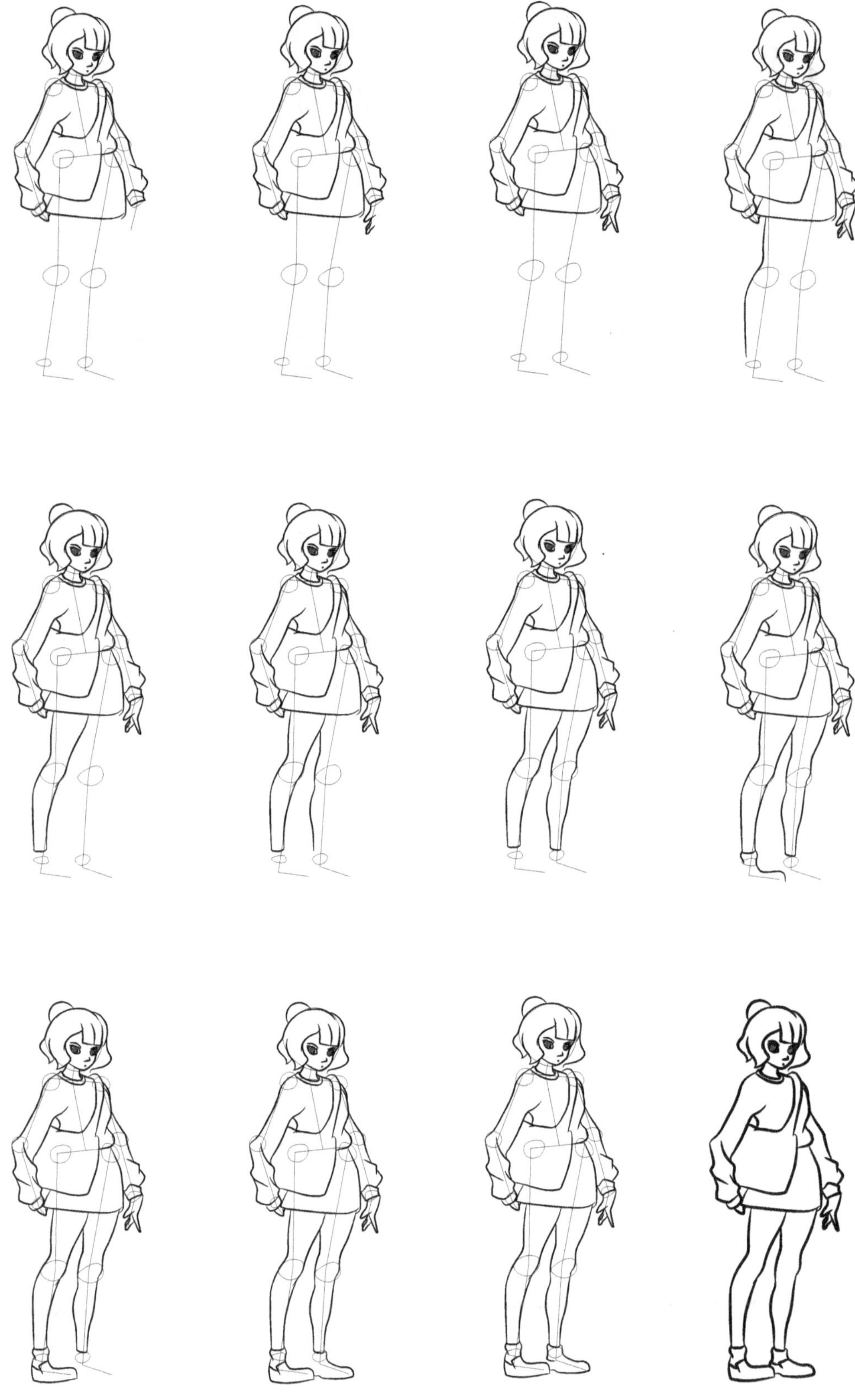

A B C D E F G H
1
2
3
4
5
6
7
8
9
10
11
12

6. To become an expert at something you may
need to spend thousands of hours doing it.
Expert artists often will often have spent more
than 10,000 hours practising.

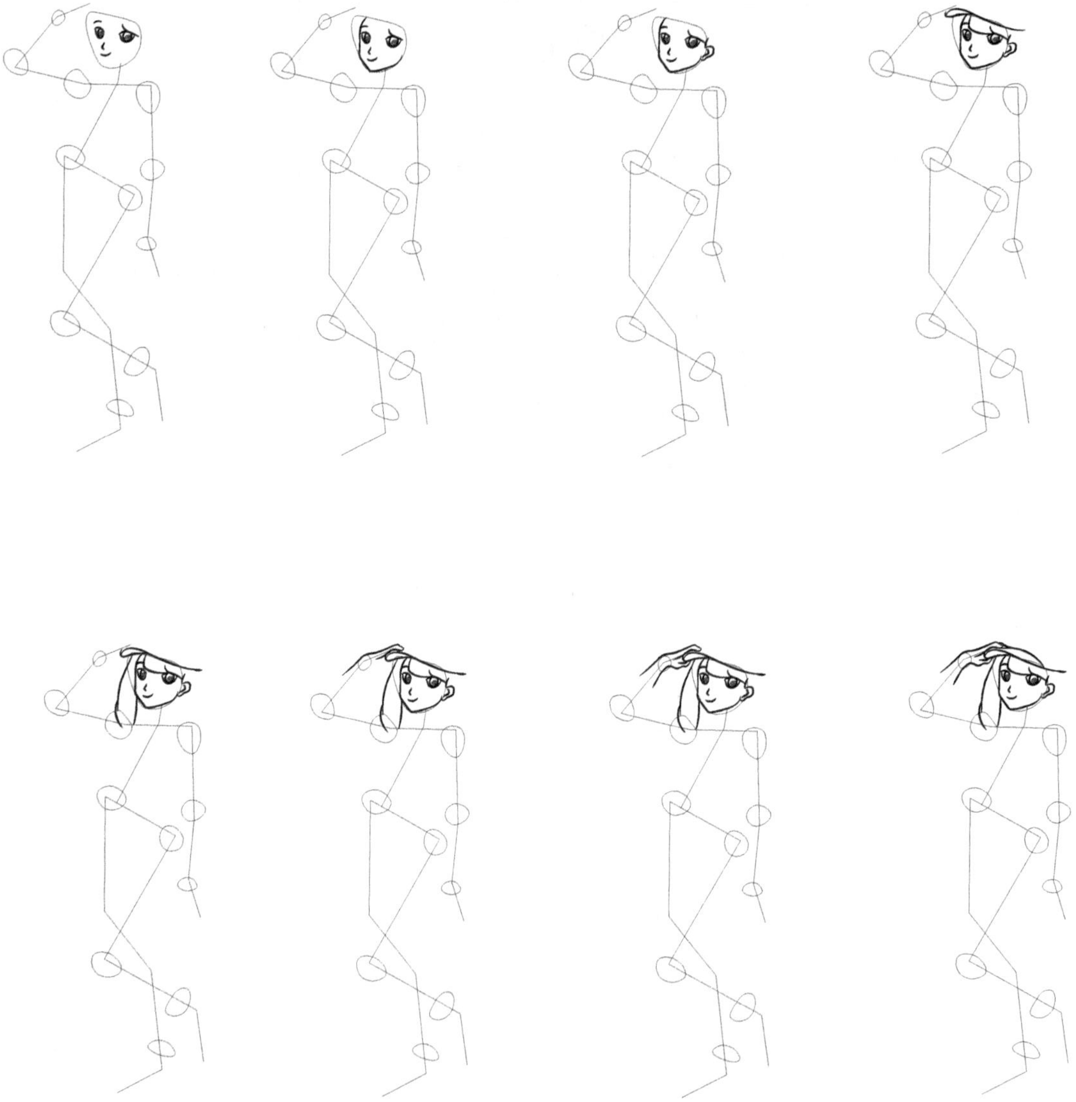

A B C D E F G H
1
2
3
4
5
6
7
8
9
10
11
12

7. If you are struggling for ideas for your work, take a break and do something different. Your mind will keep working in the background for you. Some of our greatest ideas come to us while we sleep.

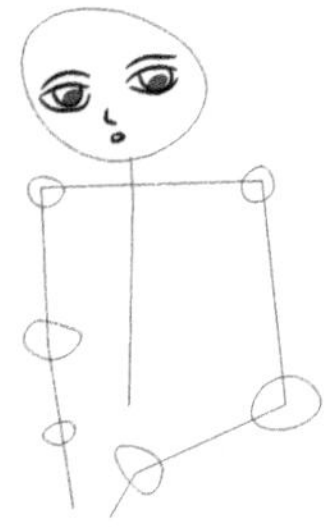

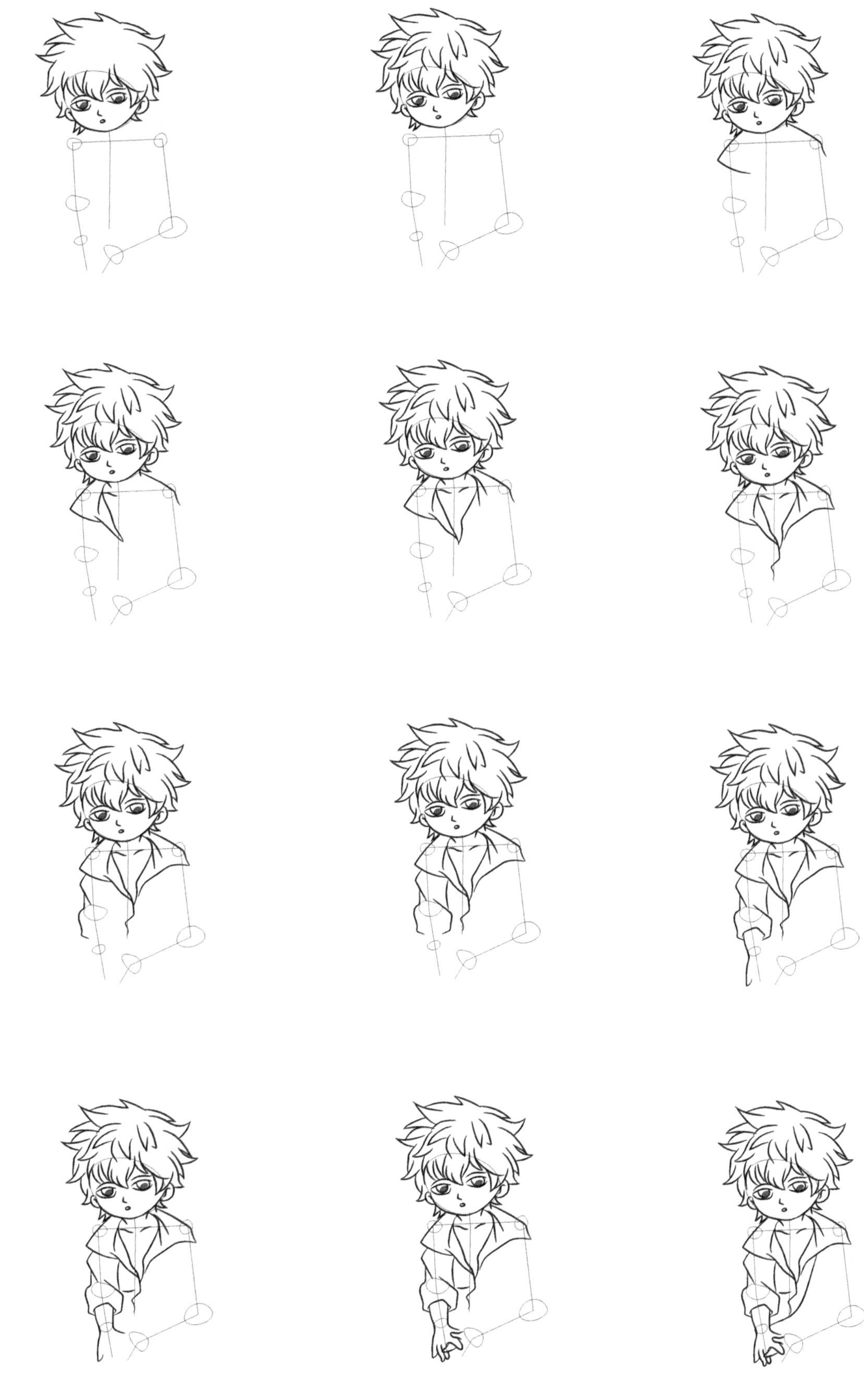

8. Many people point a finger to their head when they are thinking.

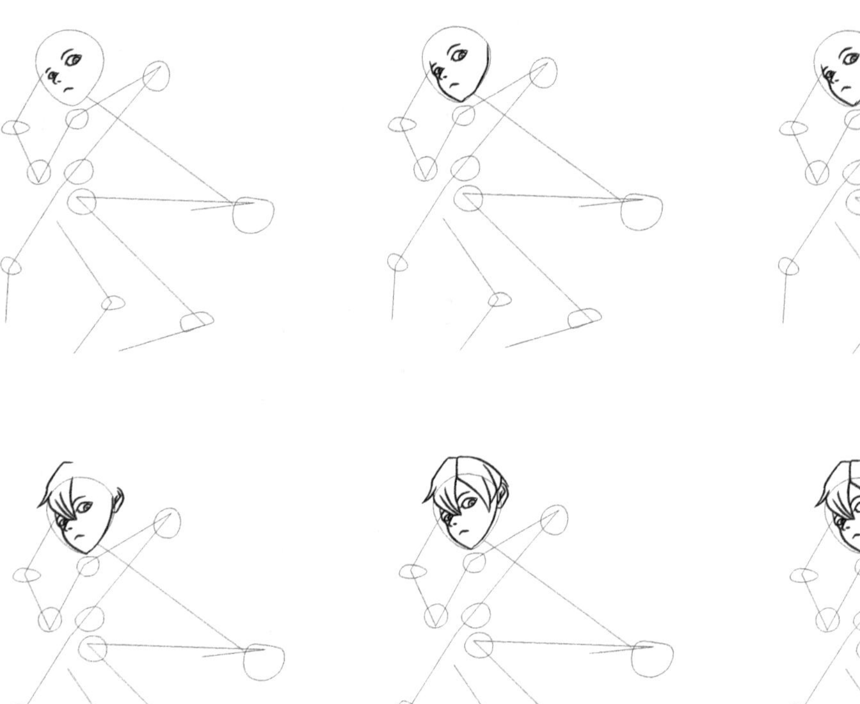

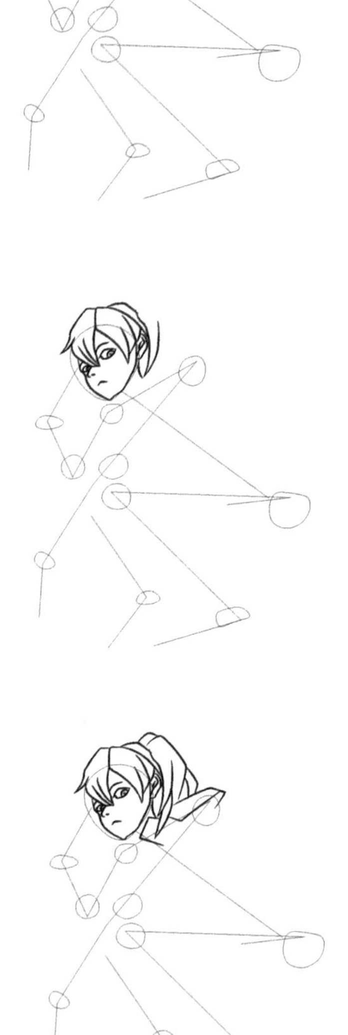

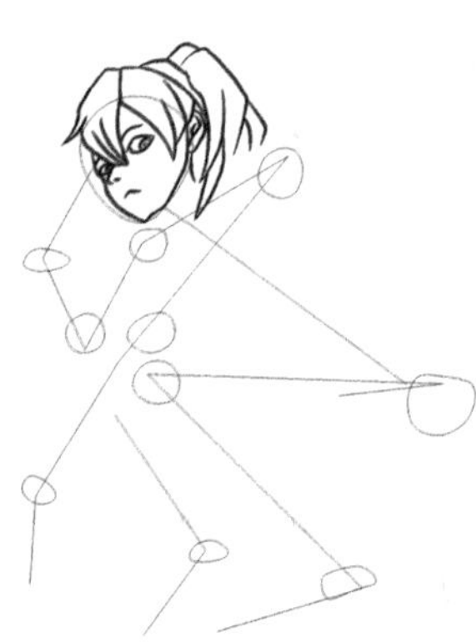

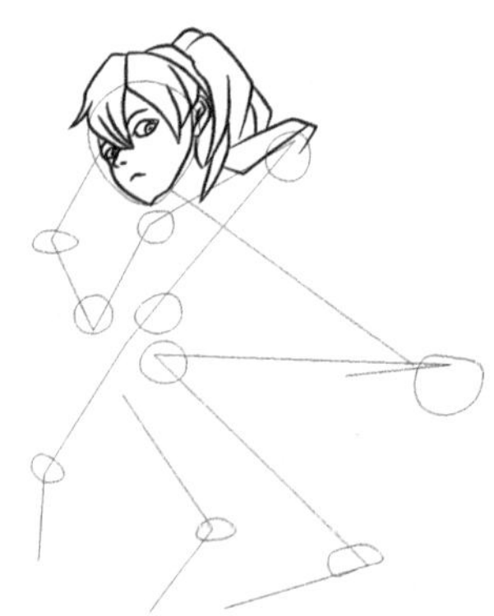

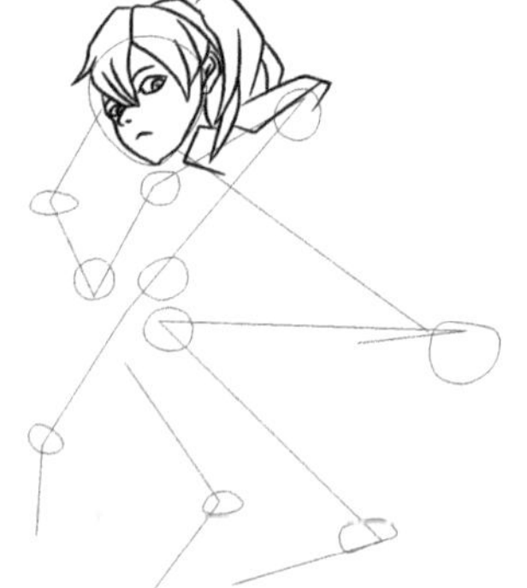

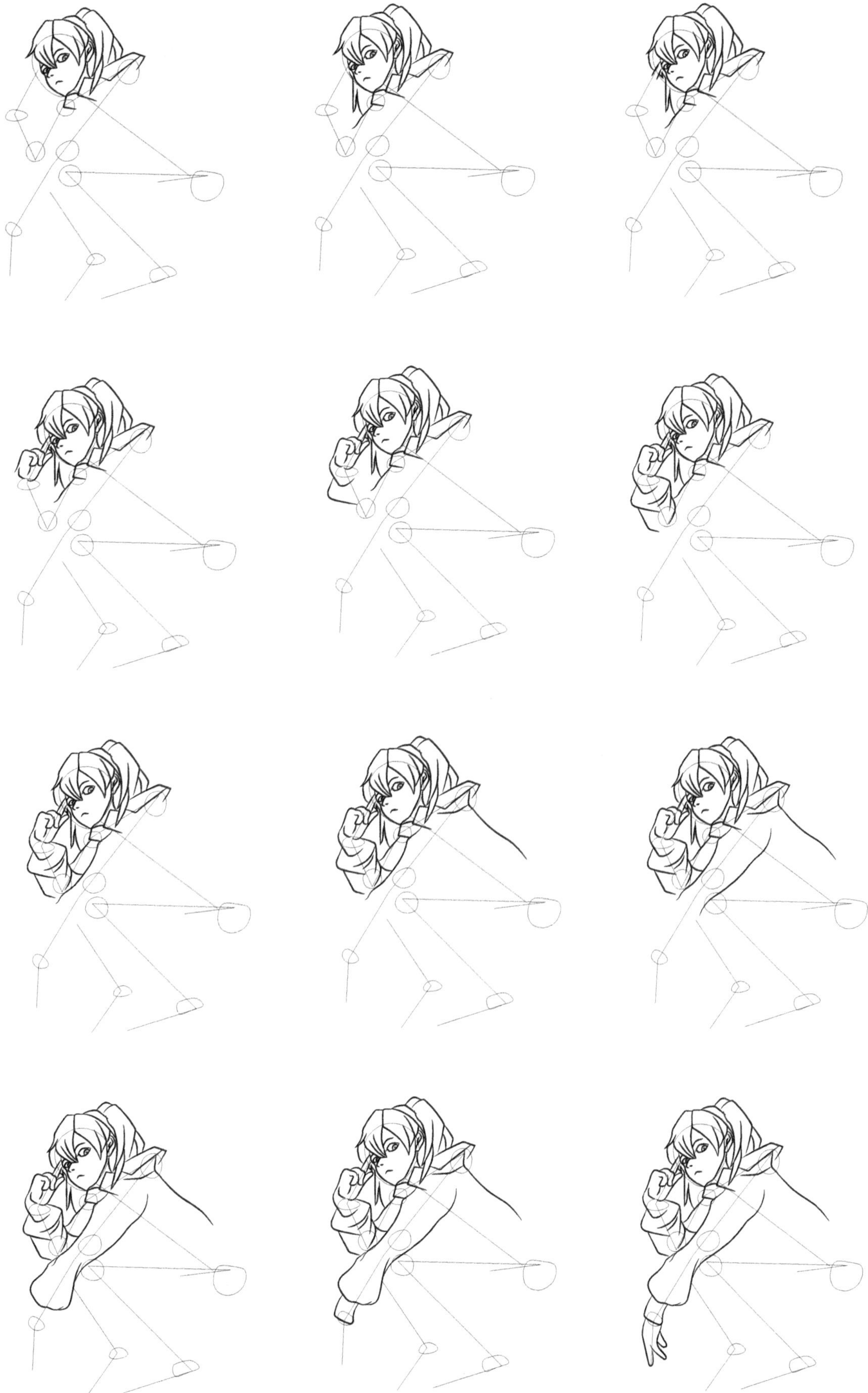

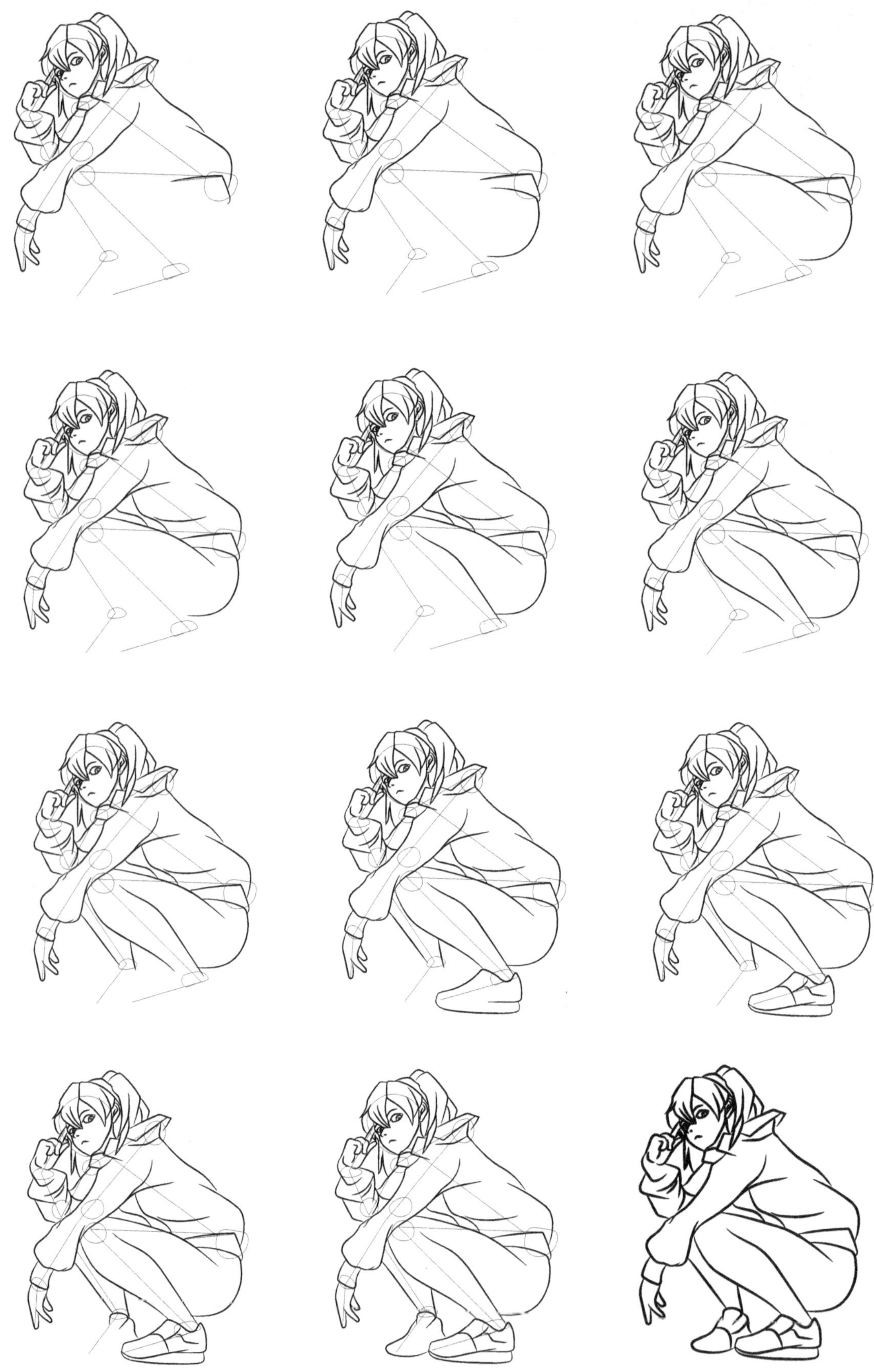

9. If you find that you are rushing, stop what you are doing and take a break. Rushing too much will reduce the quality of your work.

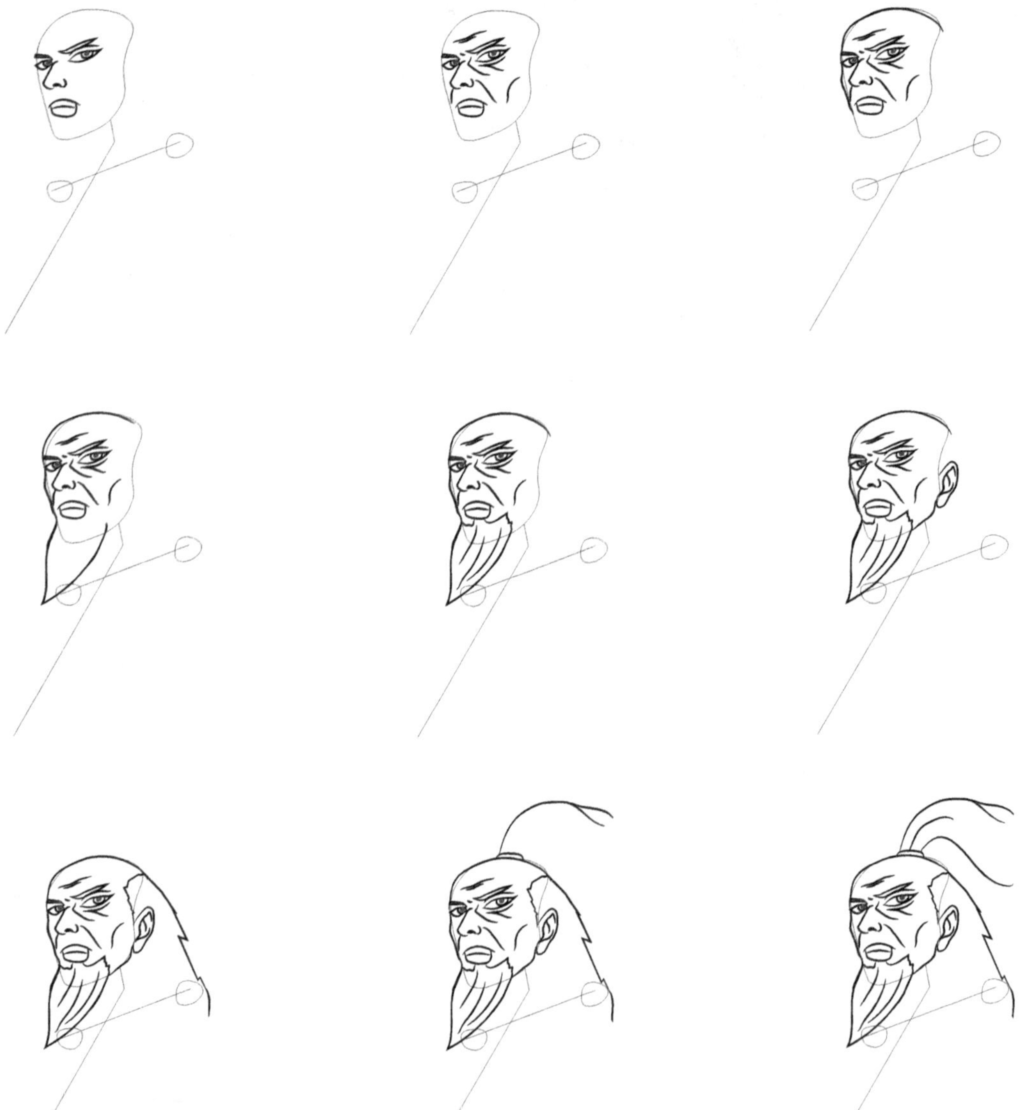

A B C D E F G H
1
2
3
4
5
6
7
8
9
10
11
12

10. To become an expert at something you may need to spend thousands of hours doing it. Expert artists often will often have spent more than 10,000 hours practising.

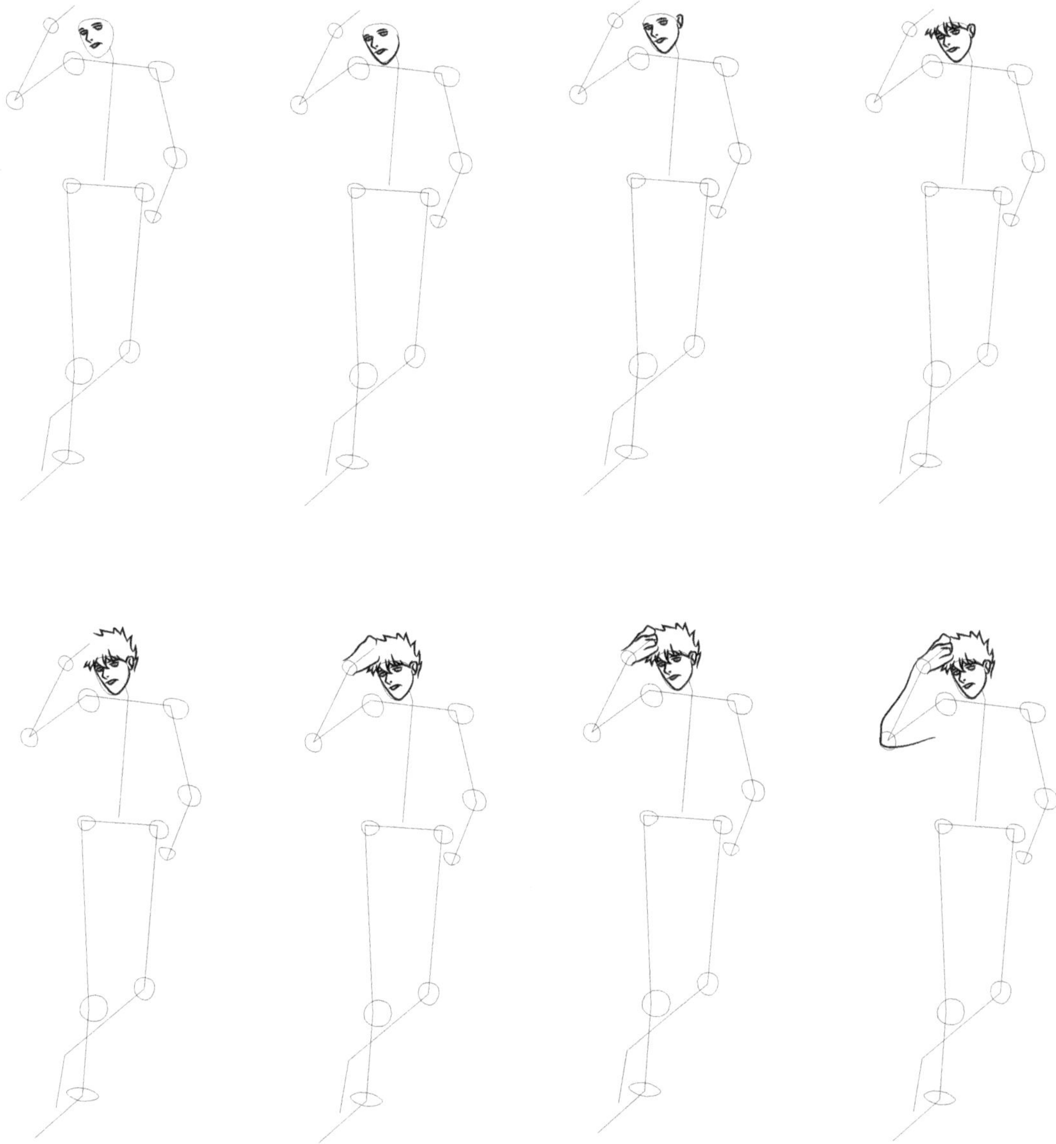

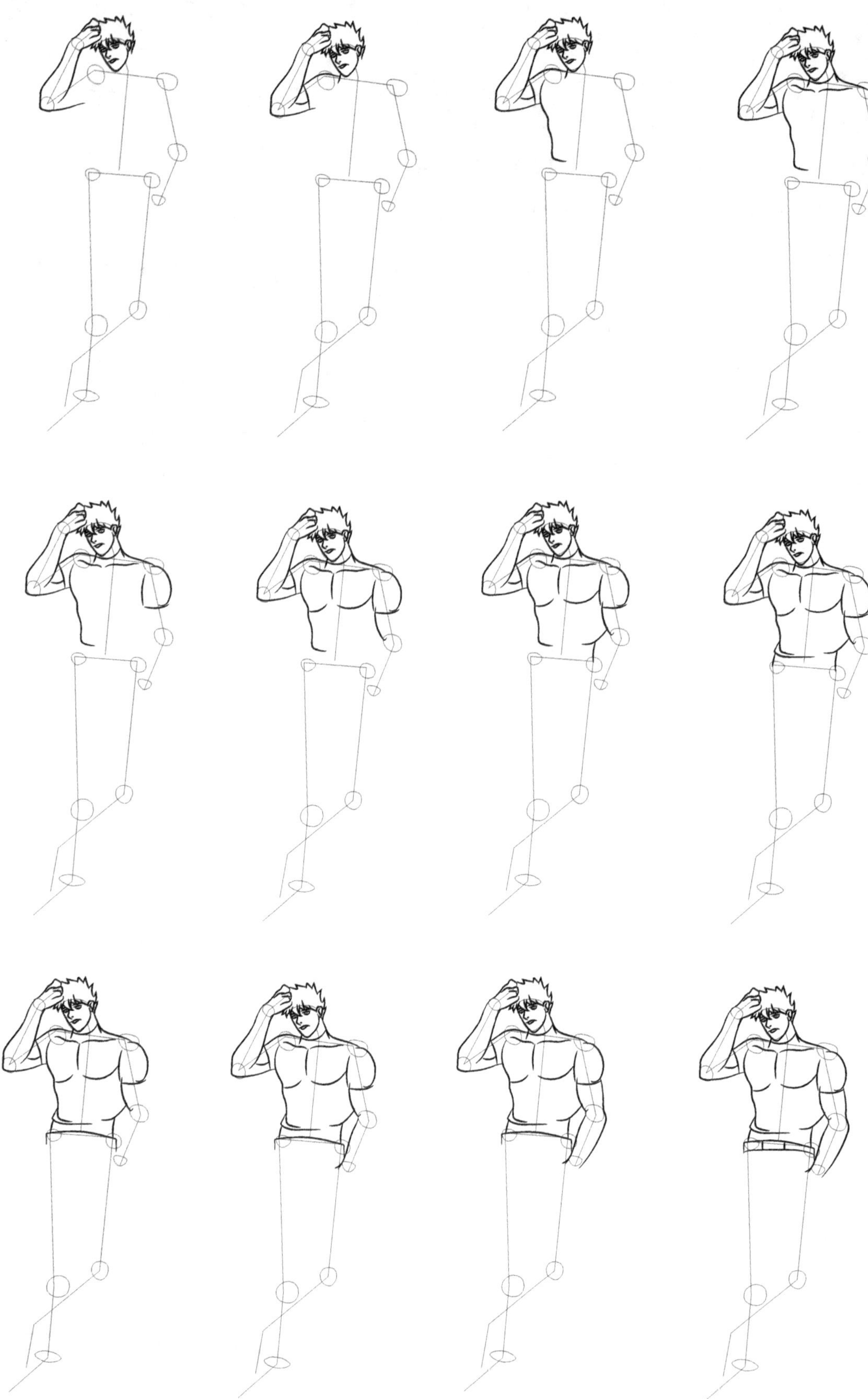

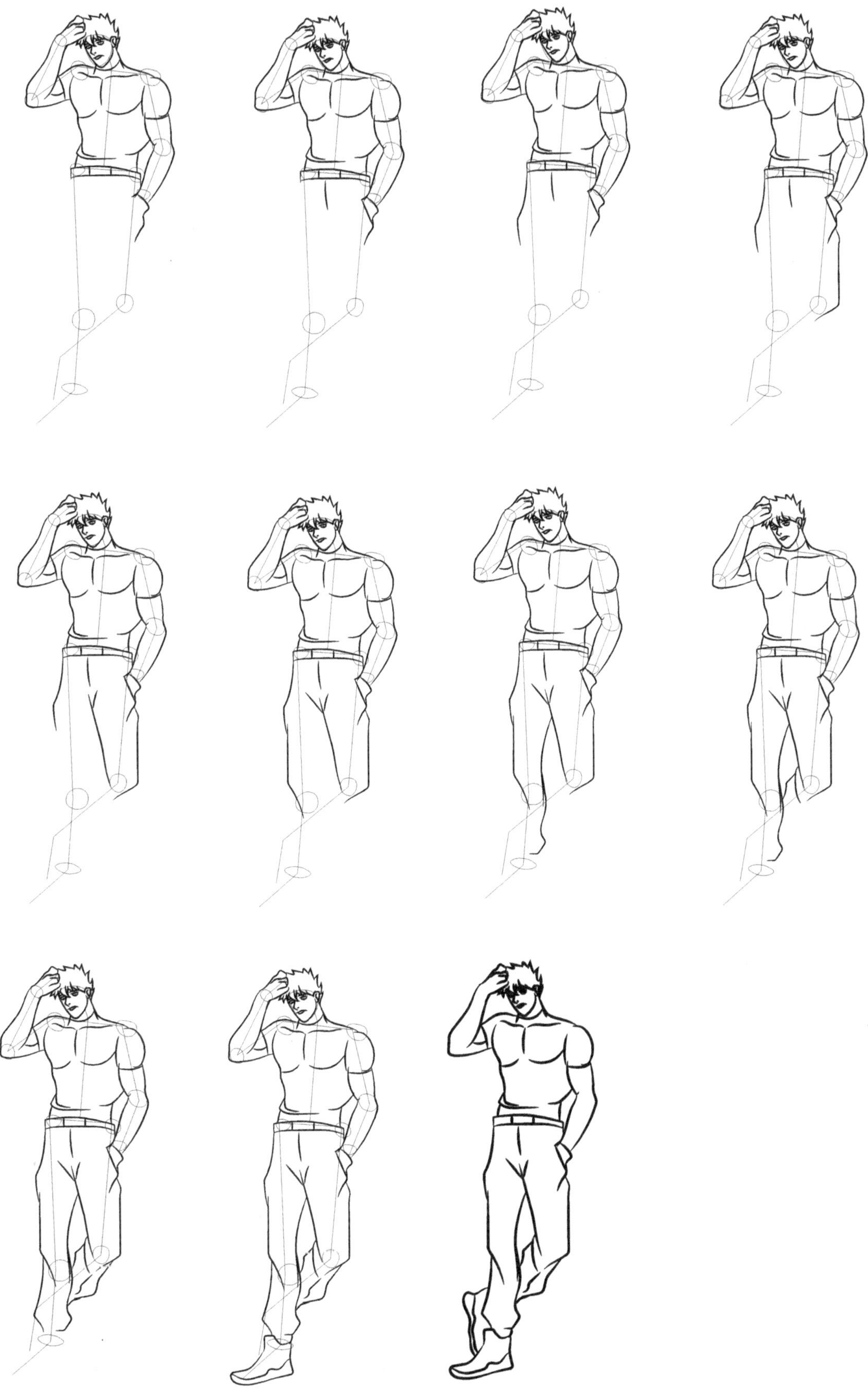

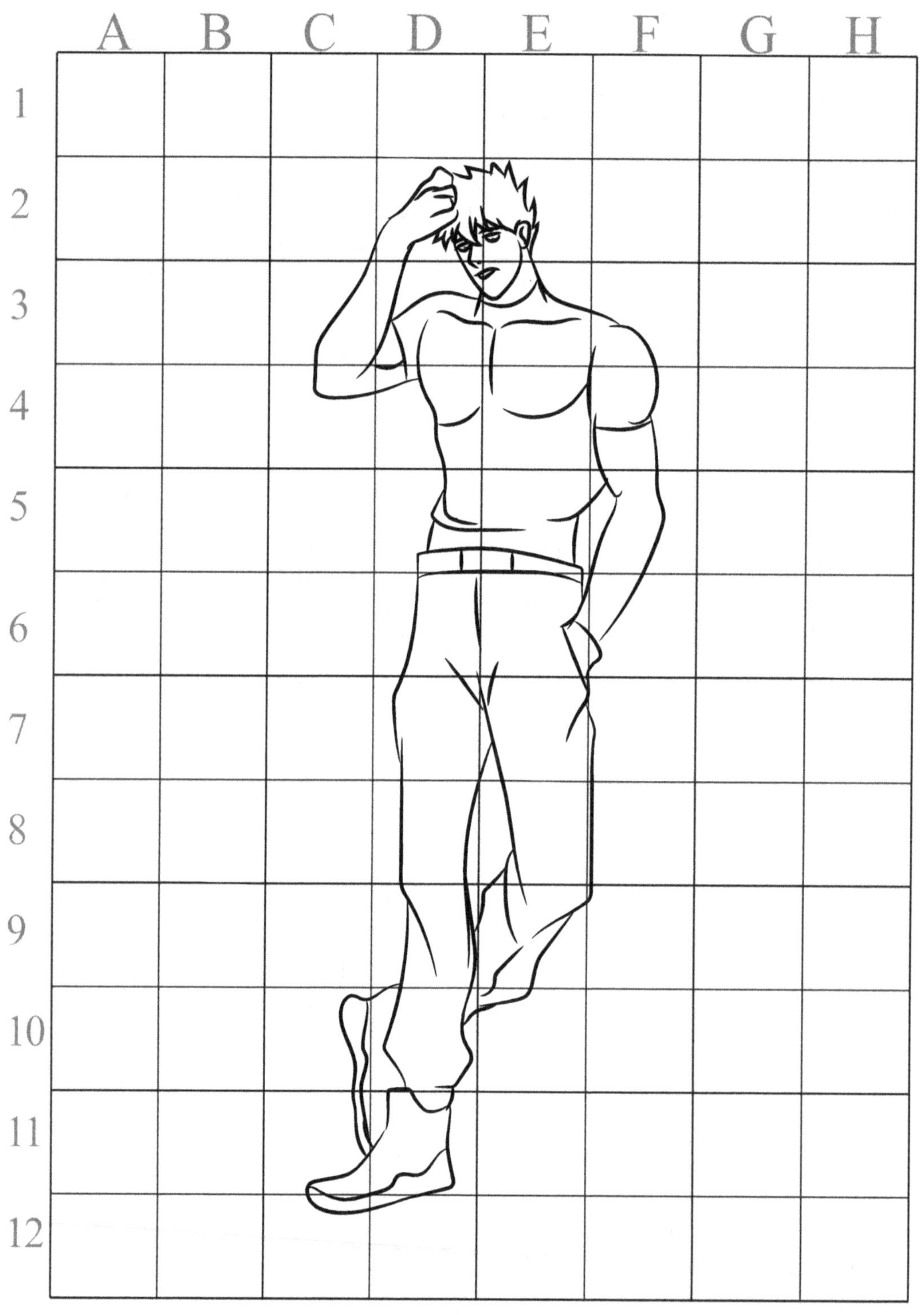

11. Your character may have a basic shape that you can attempt to outline using your initial grid.

12. Adjusting the pressure you place on
your pencil will help you vary the
thickness of your lines.

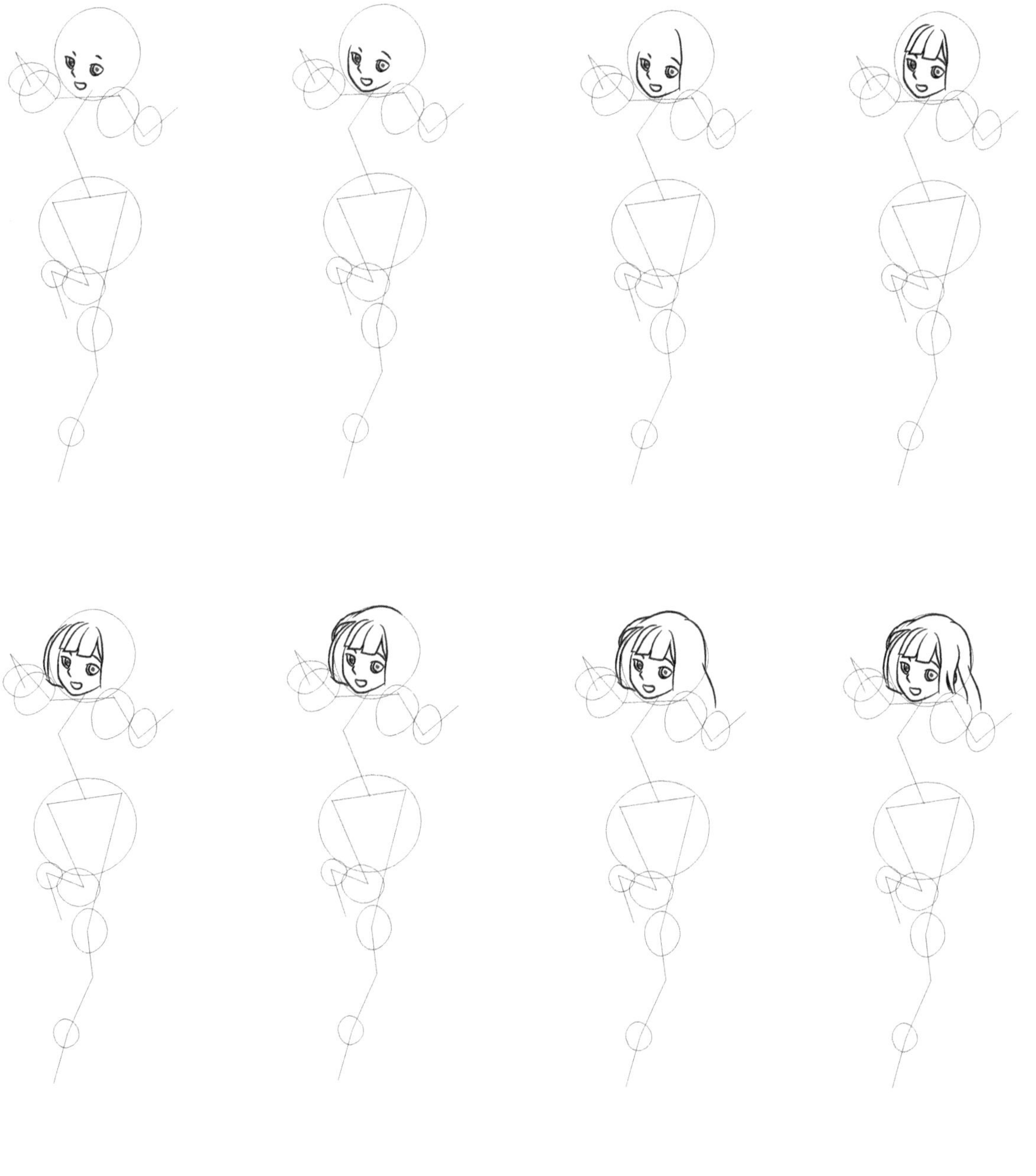

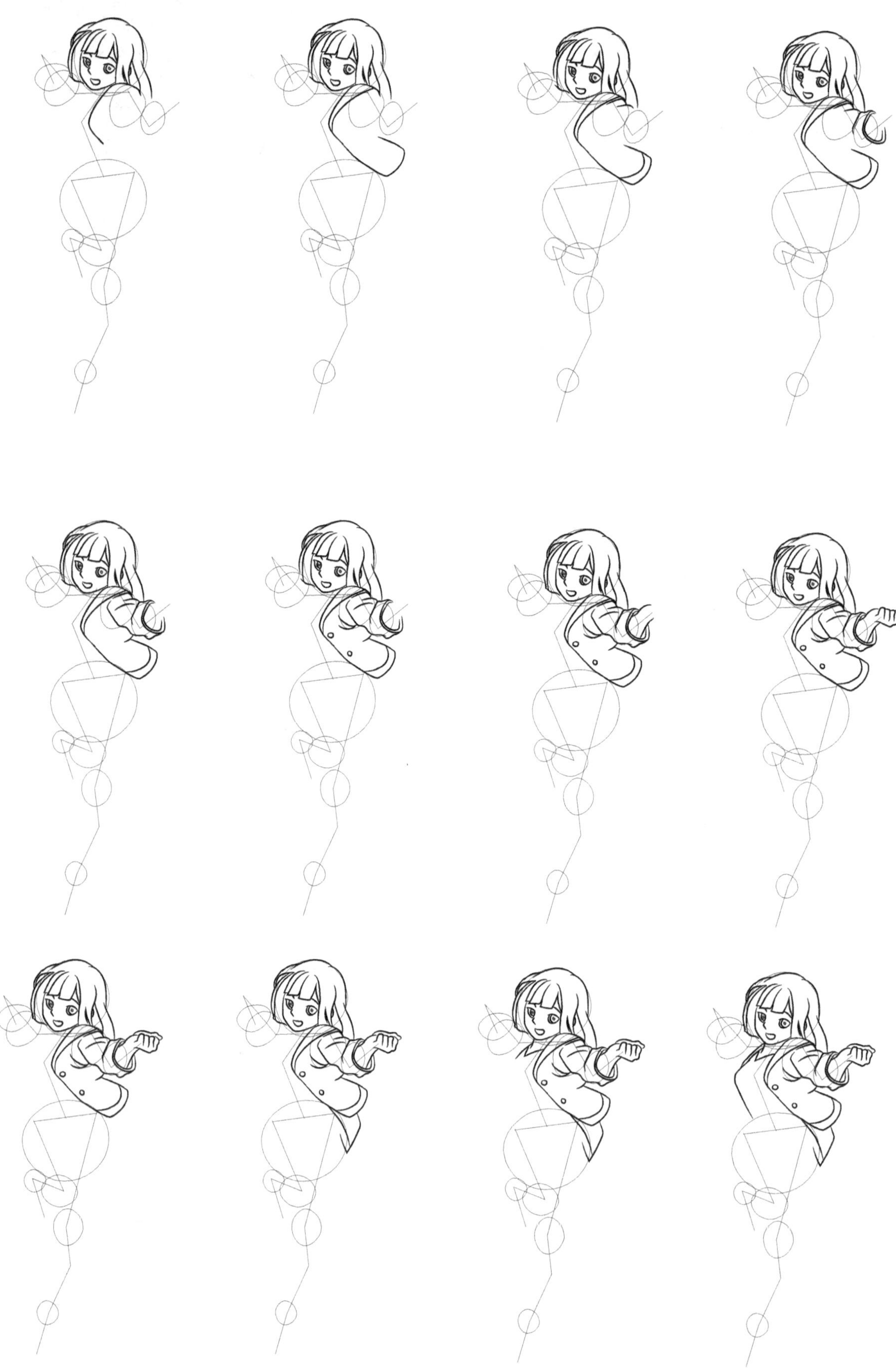

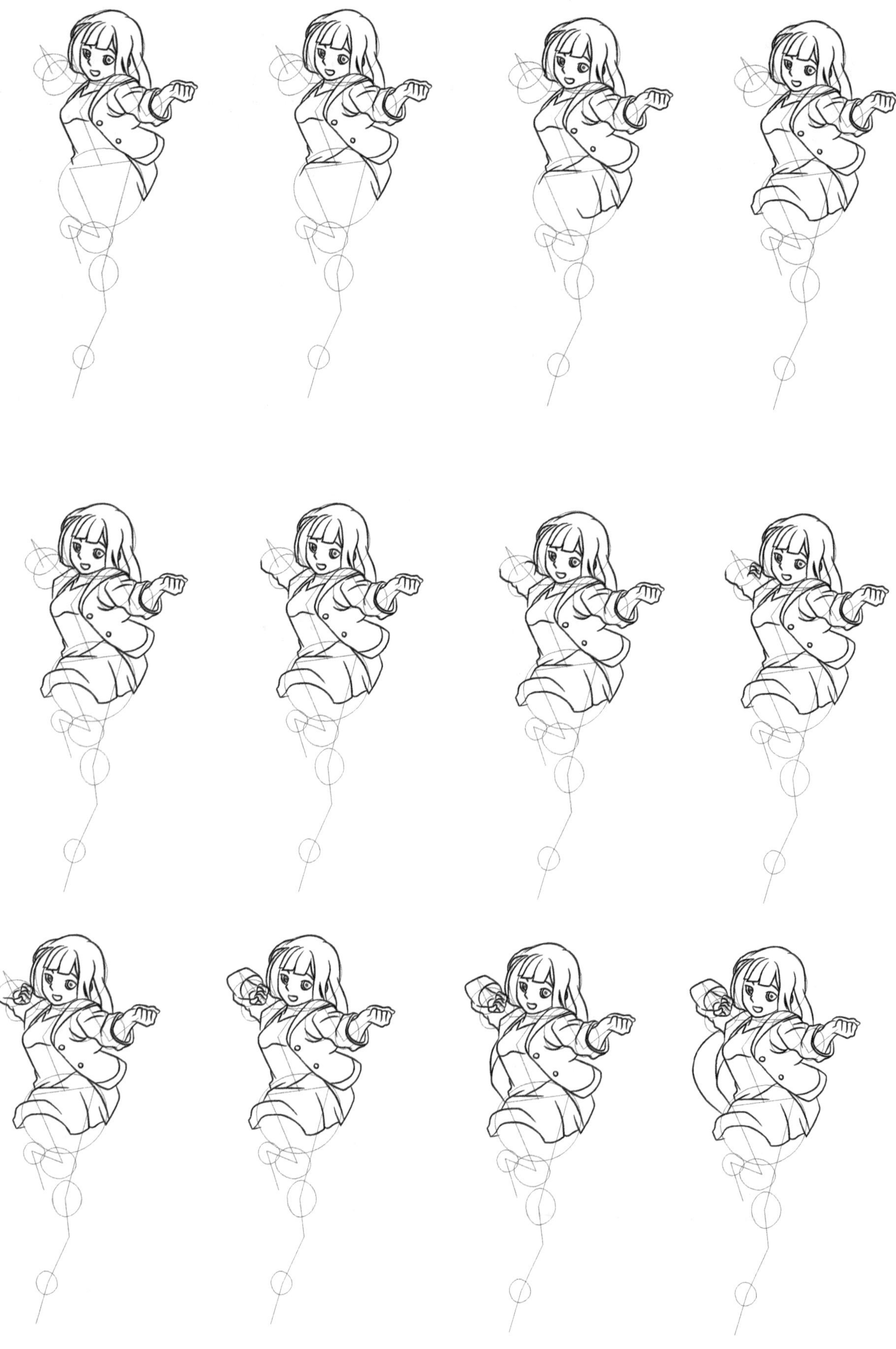

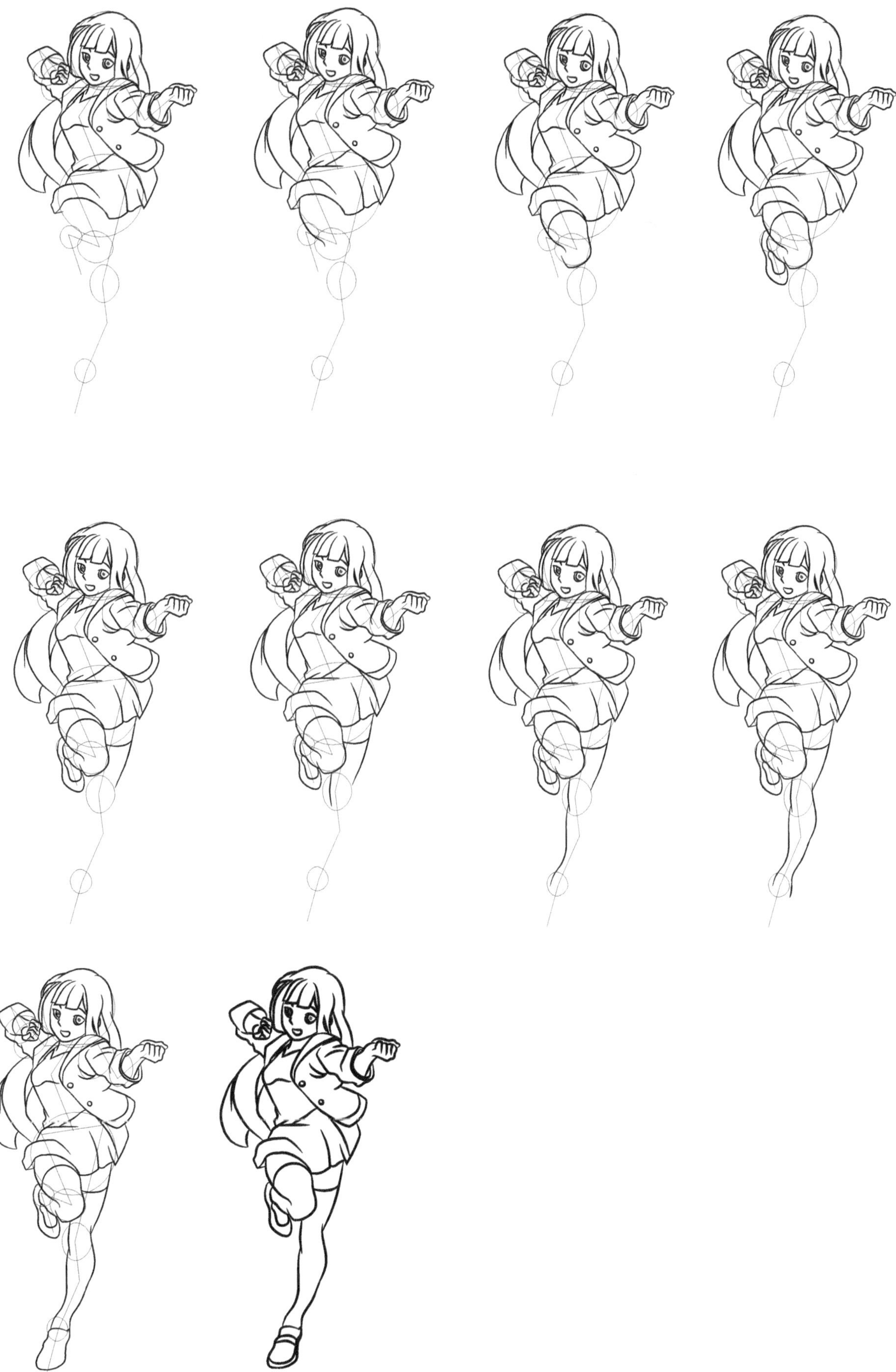

A B C D E F G H
1
2
3
4
5
6
7
8
9
10
11
12

13. More complex characters require a lot more planning. One small step at time is the best approach to take, as all of those steps will add up.

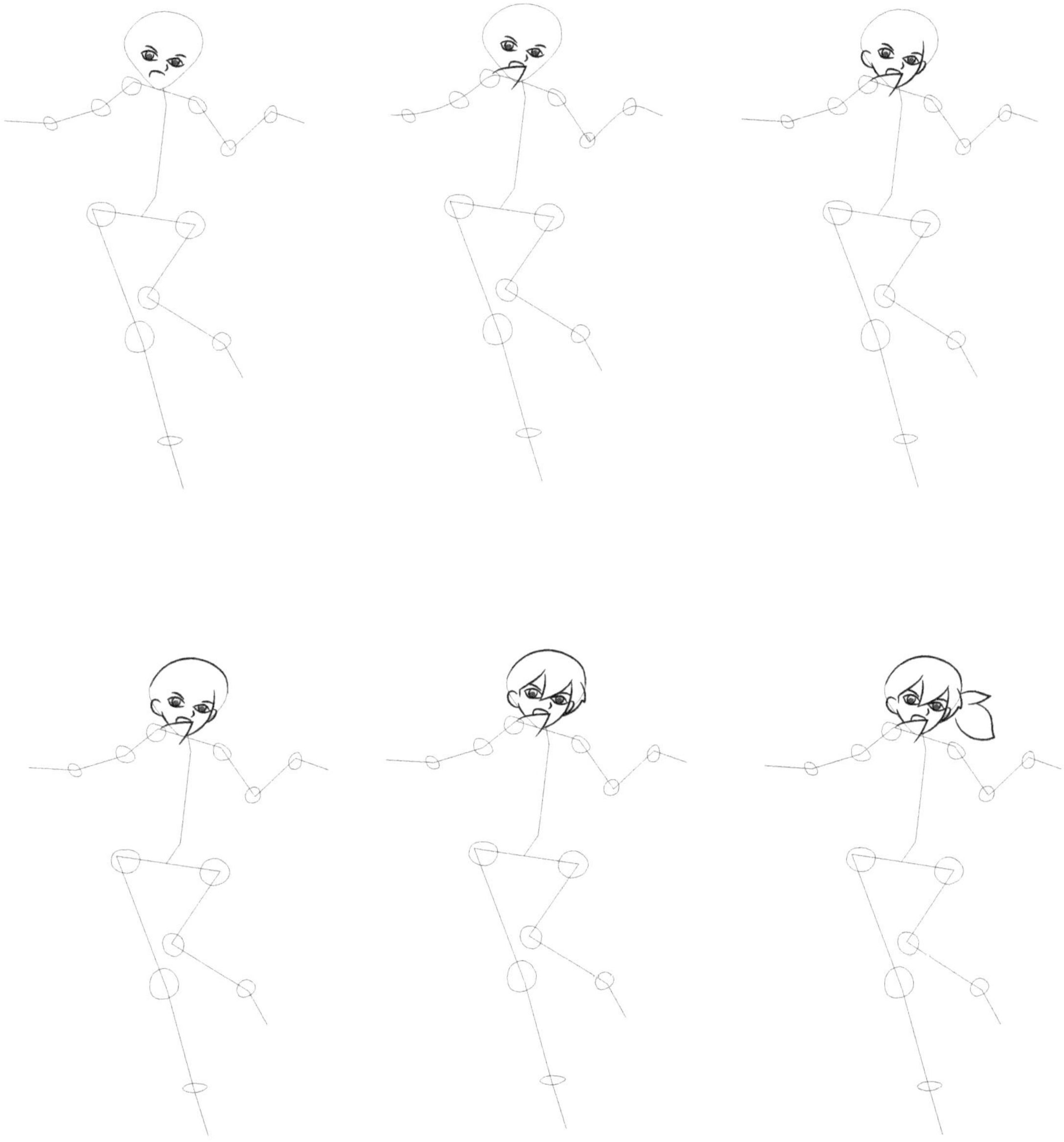

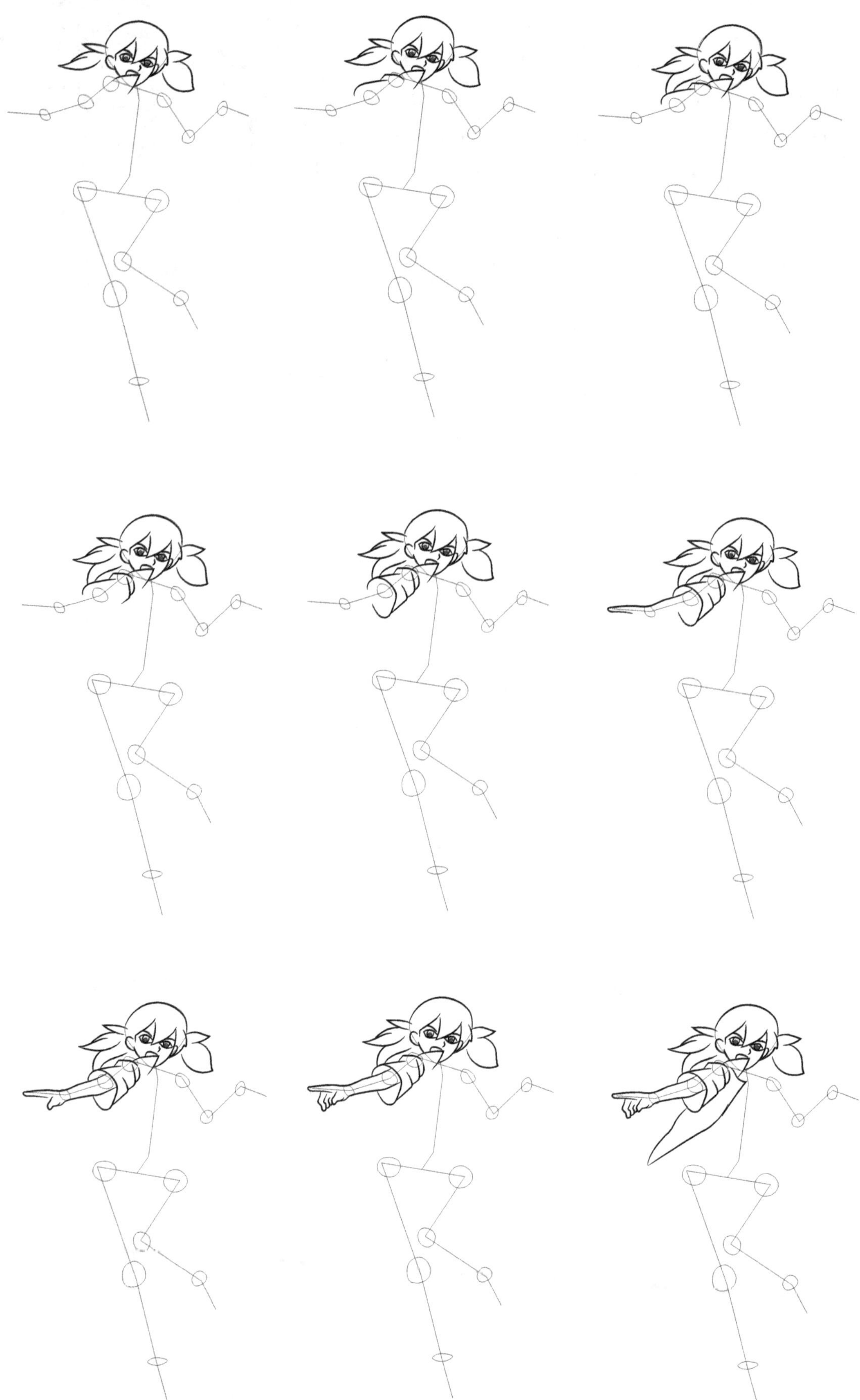

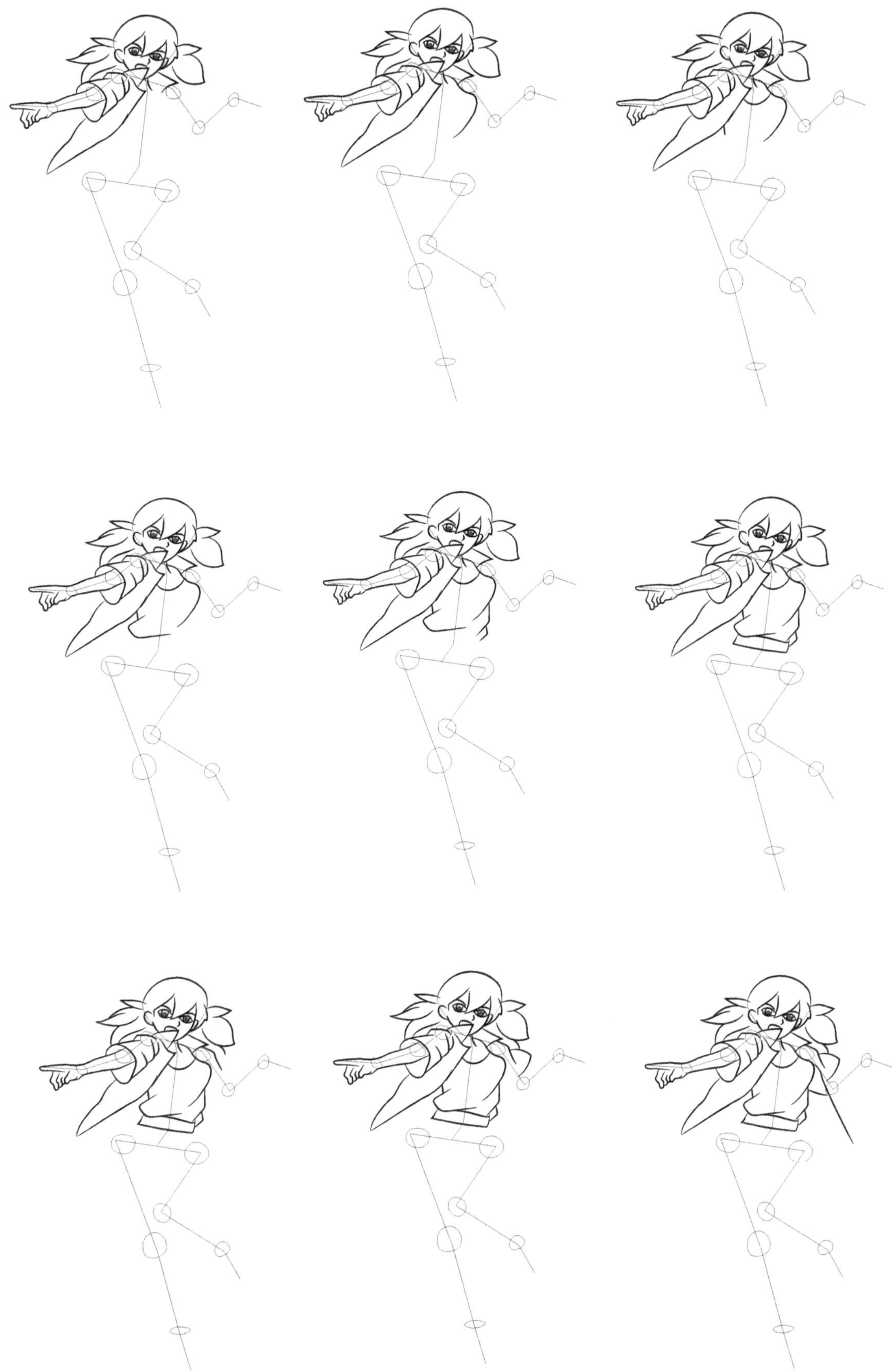

14. Many people leave their index finger
pointing outwards when they have an idea
that they want to express.

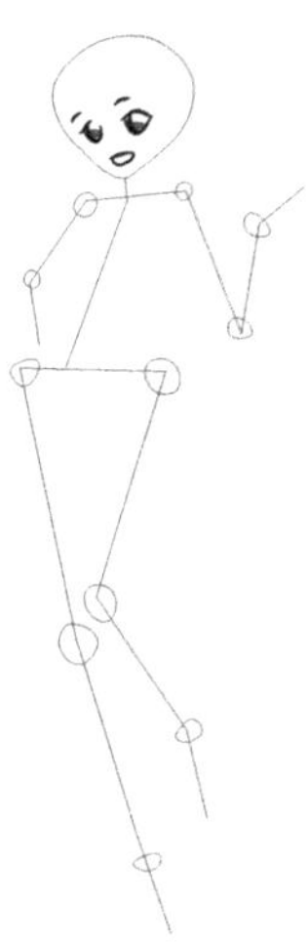

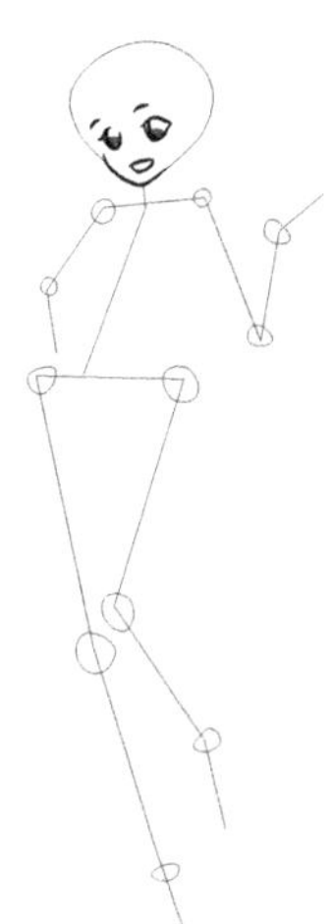

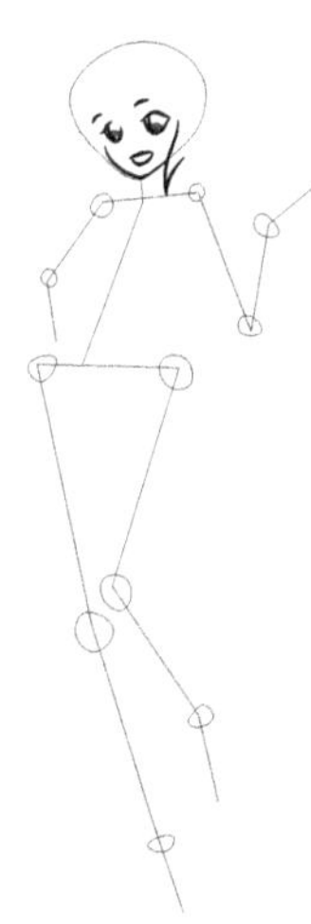

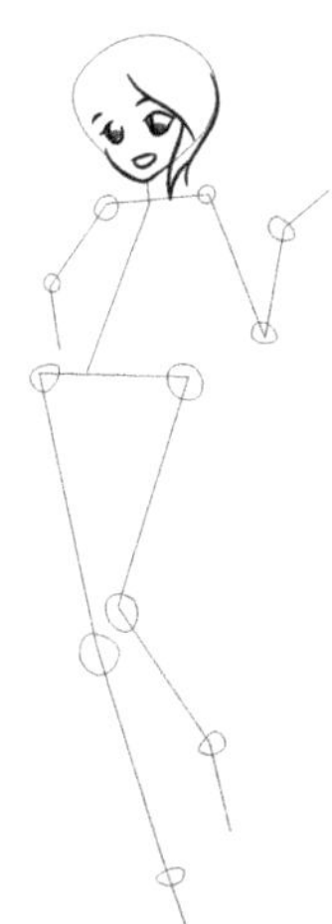

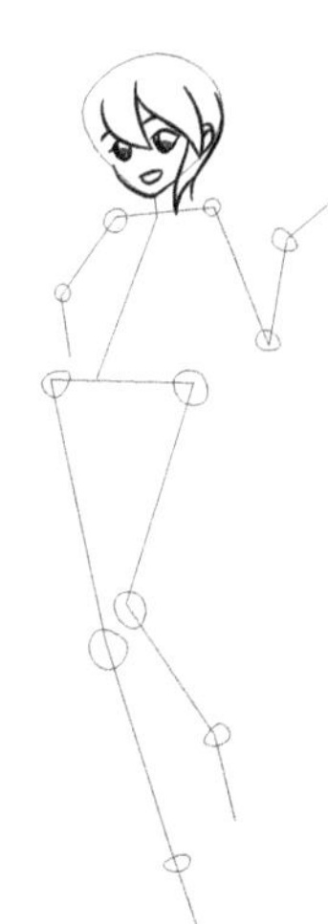

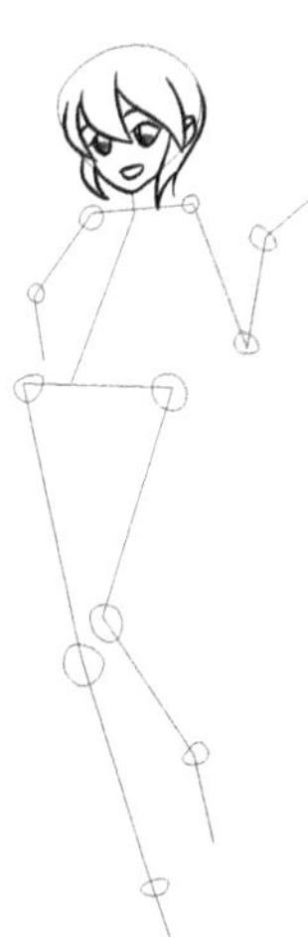

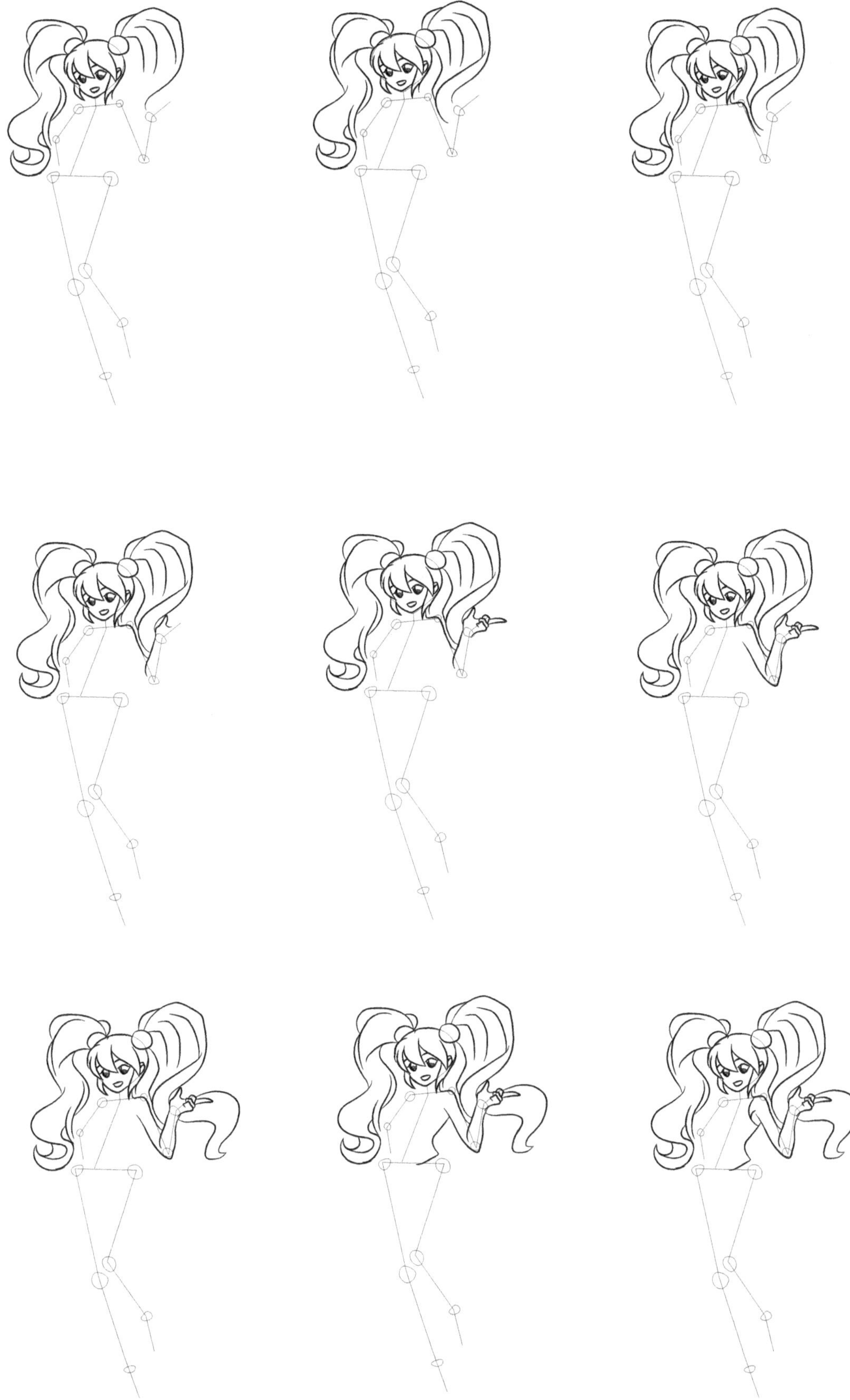

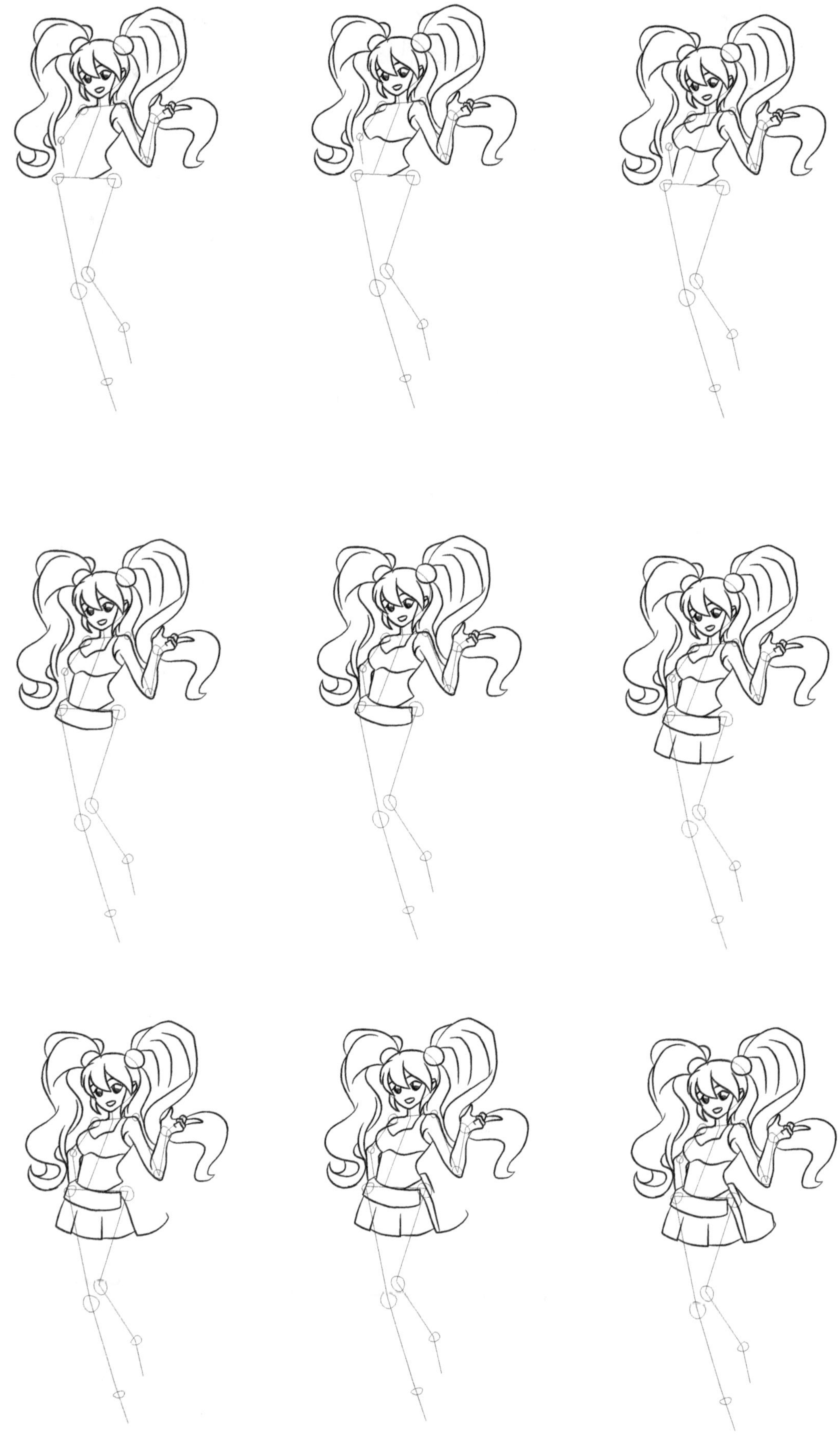

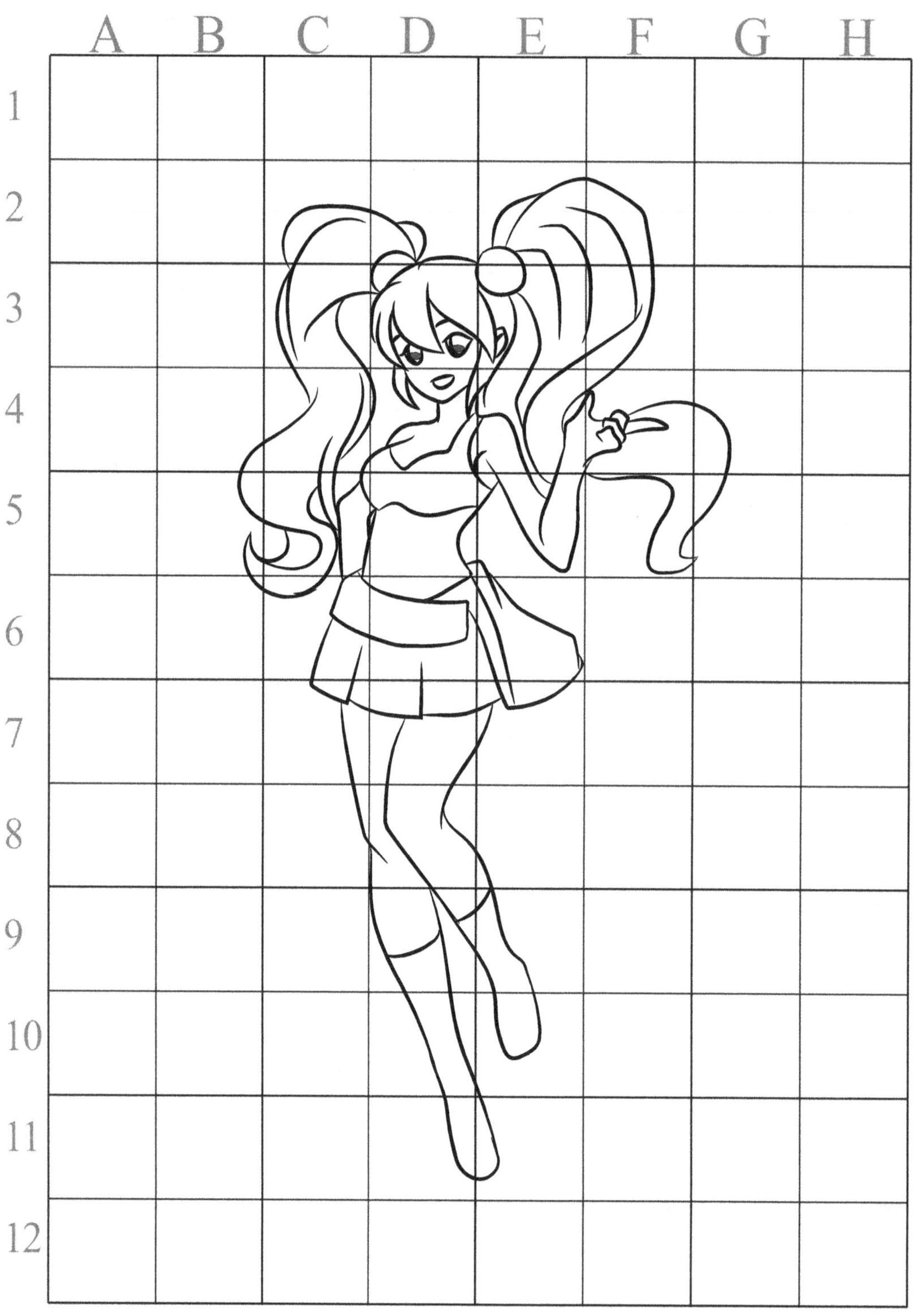

15. Drawing your character with thumbs raised and with hands open suggests your character is expressing something in a confident and open way.

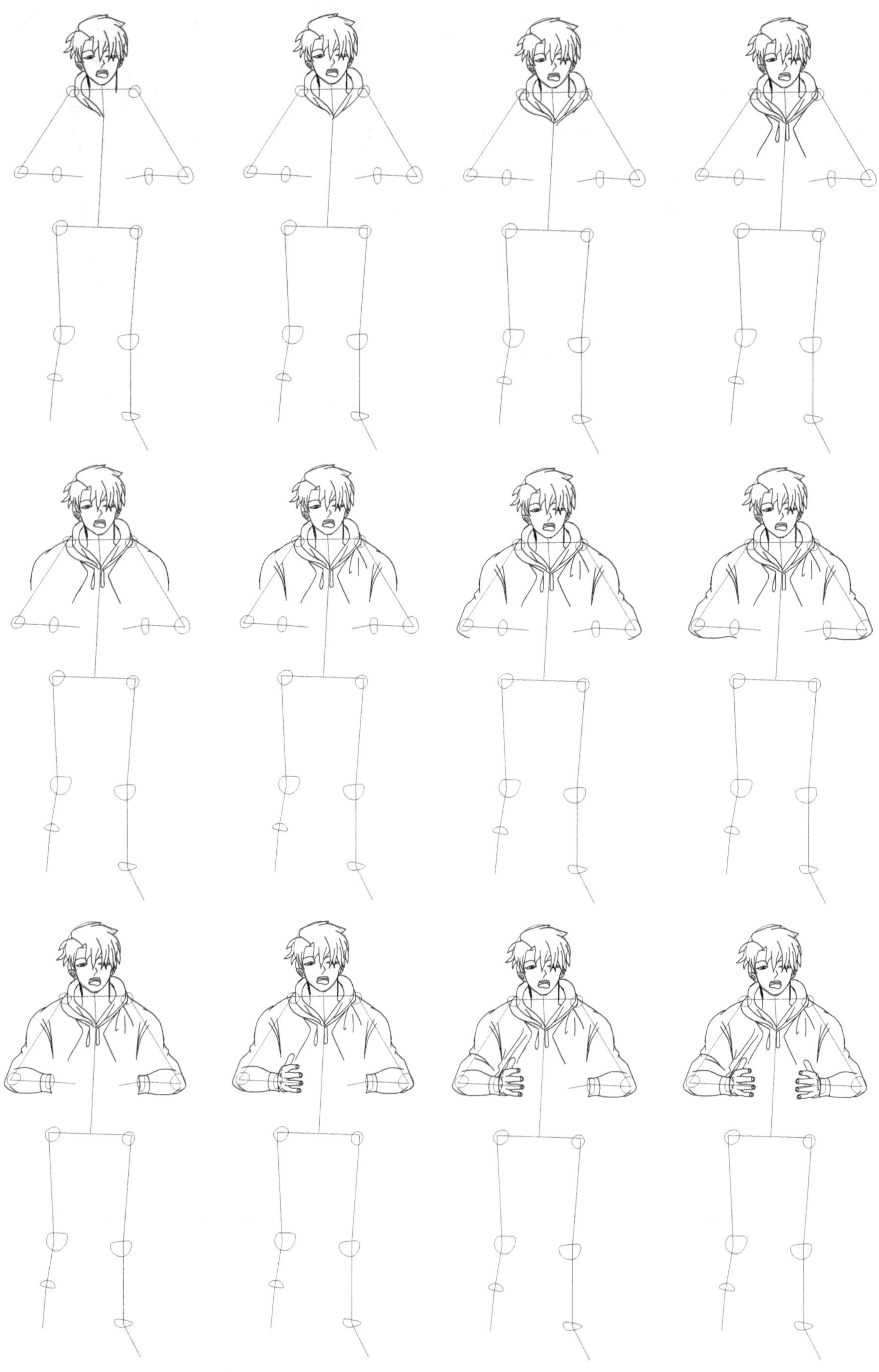

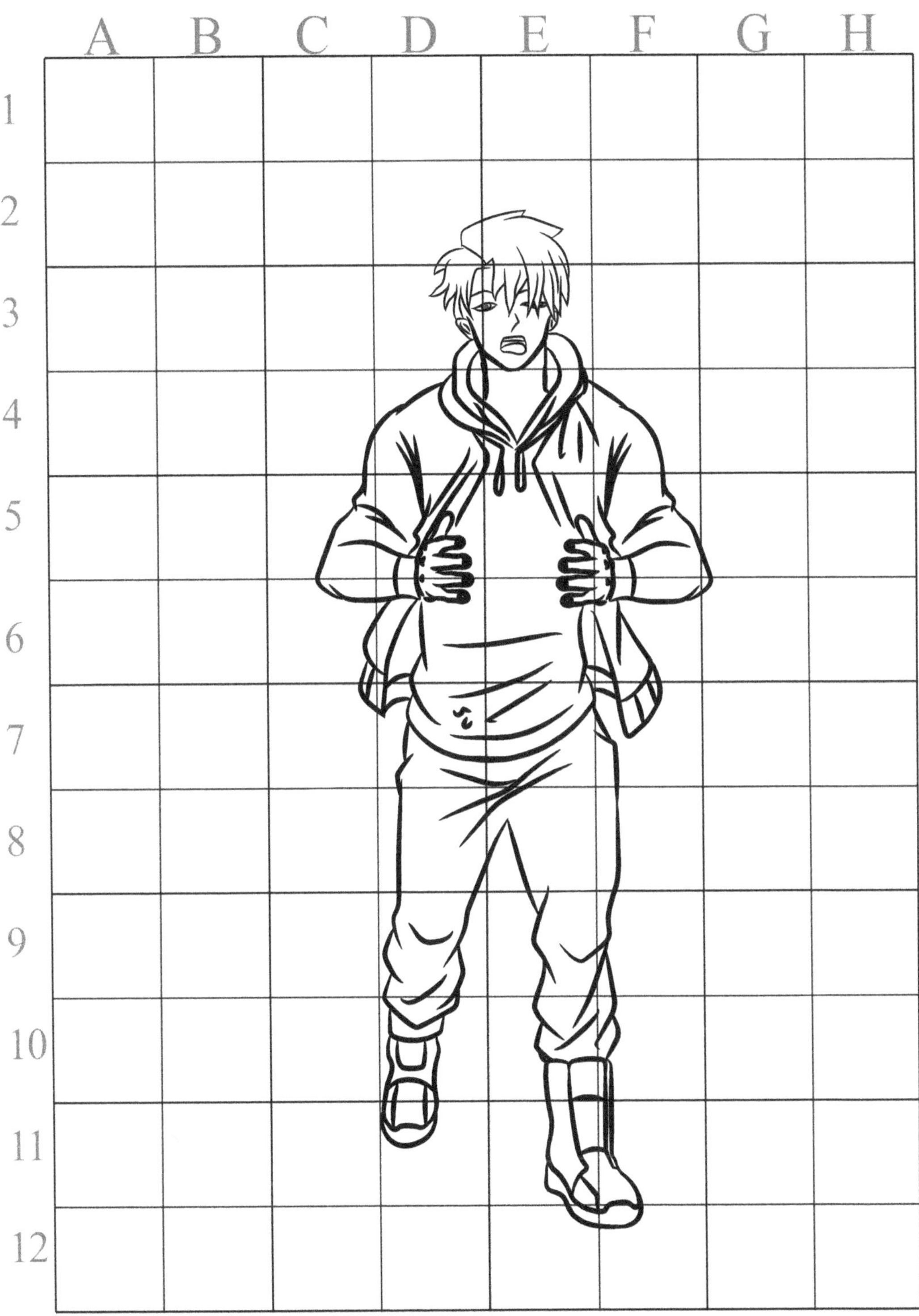

16. Drawing your character with one hand
open with the index finger raised and the
other hand made into a clenched fist suggests
that your character is open about a point they
wish to raise but will follow up openness with
aggression if necessary.

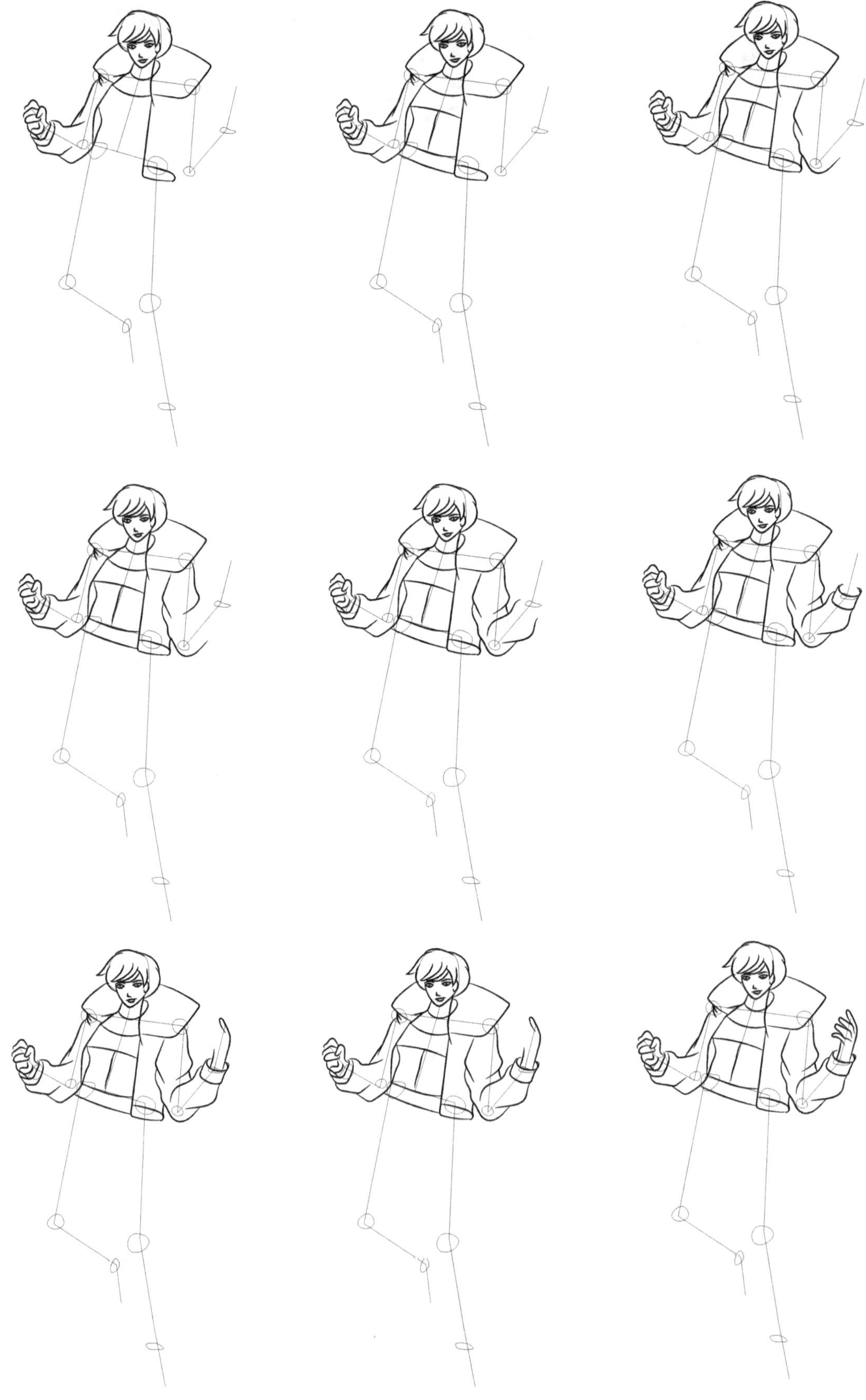

17. If your characters are carrying something heavy their posture will need to be adjusted to show this. Bending the knees shows even weight distribution and lowers the centre of gravity. This creates greater stability.

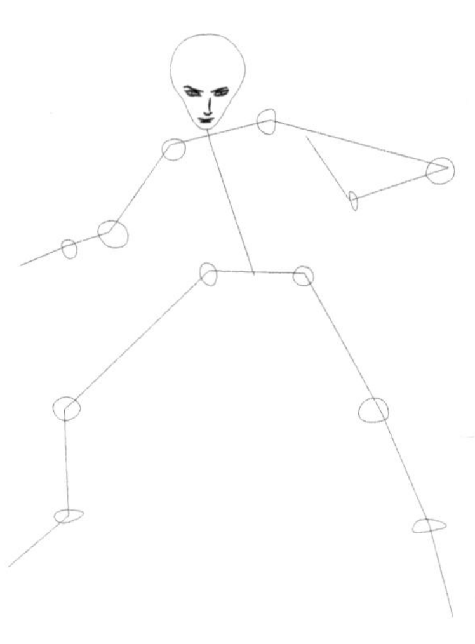

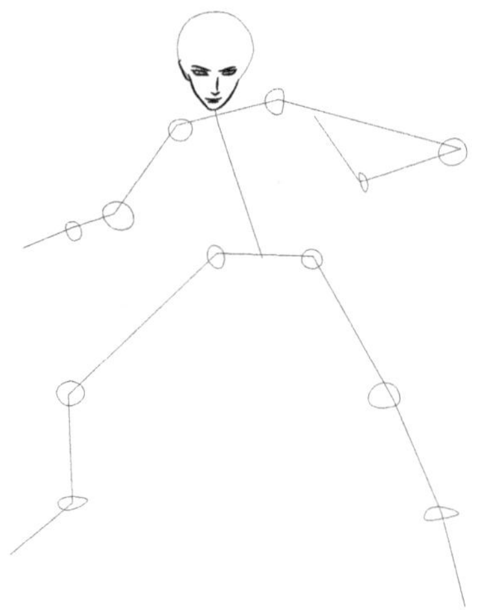

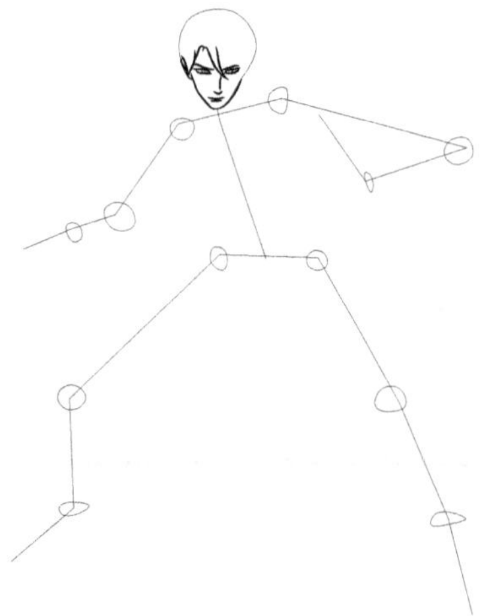

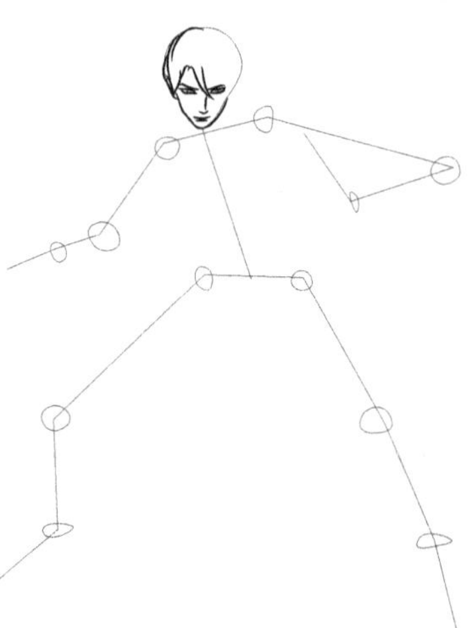

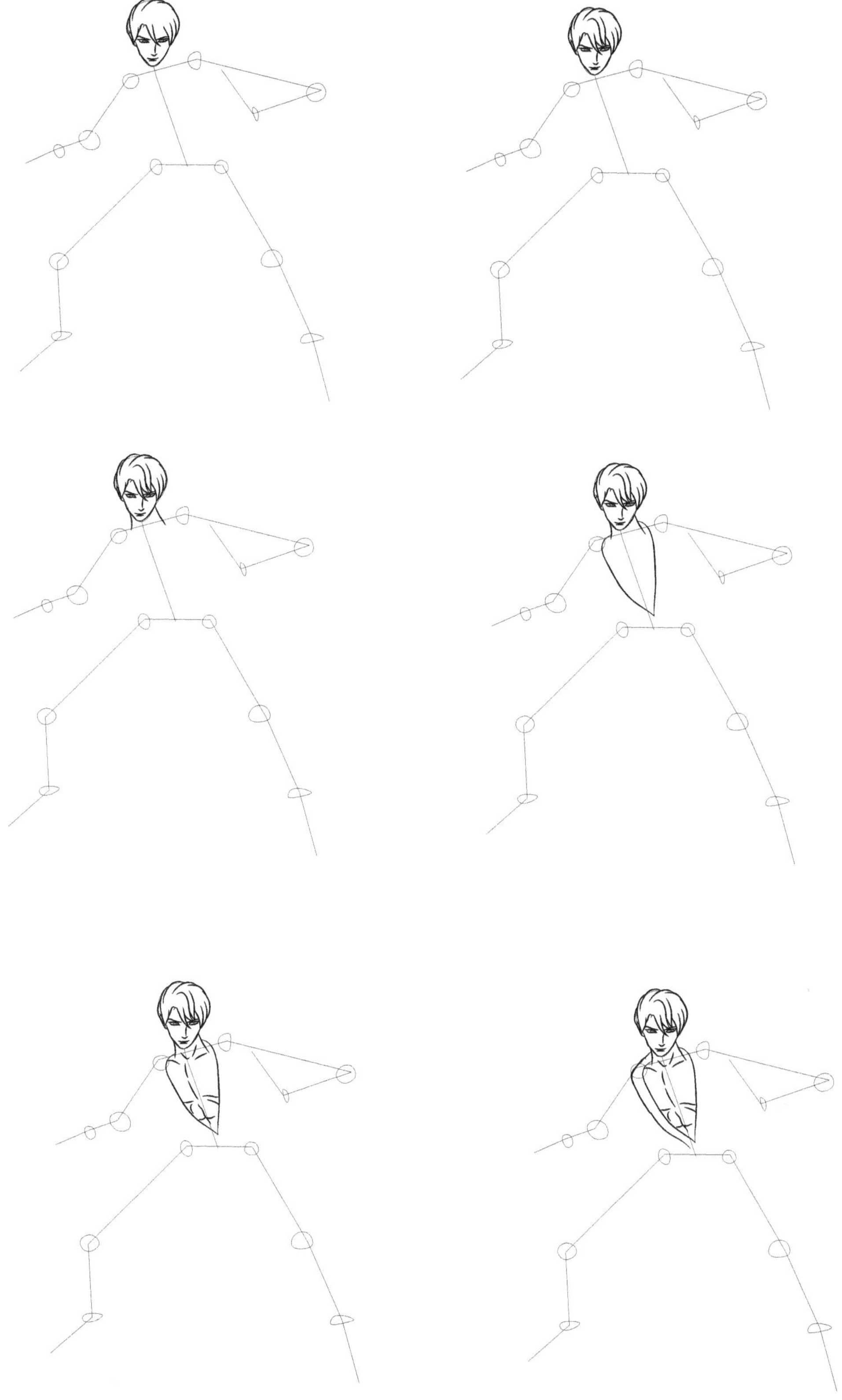

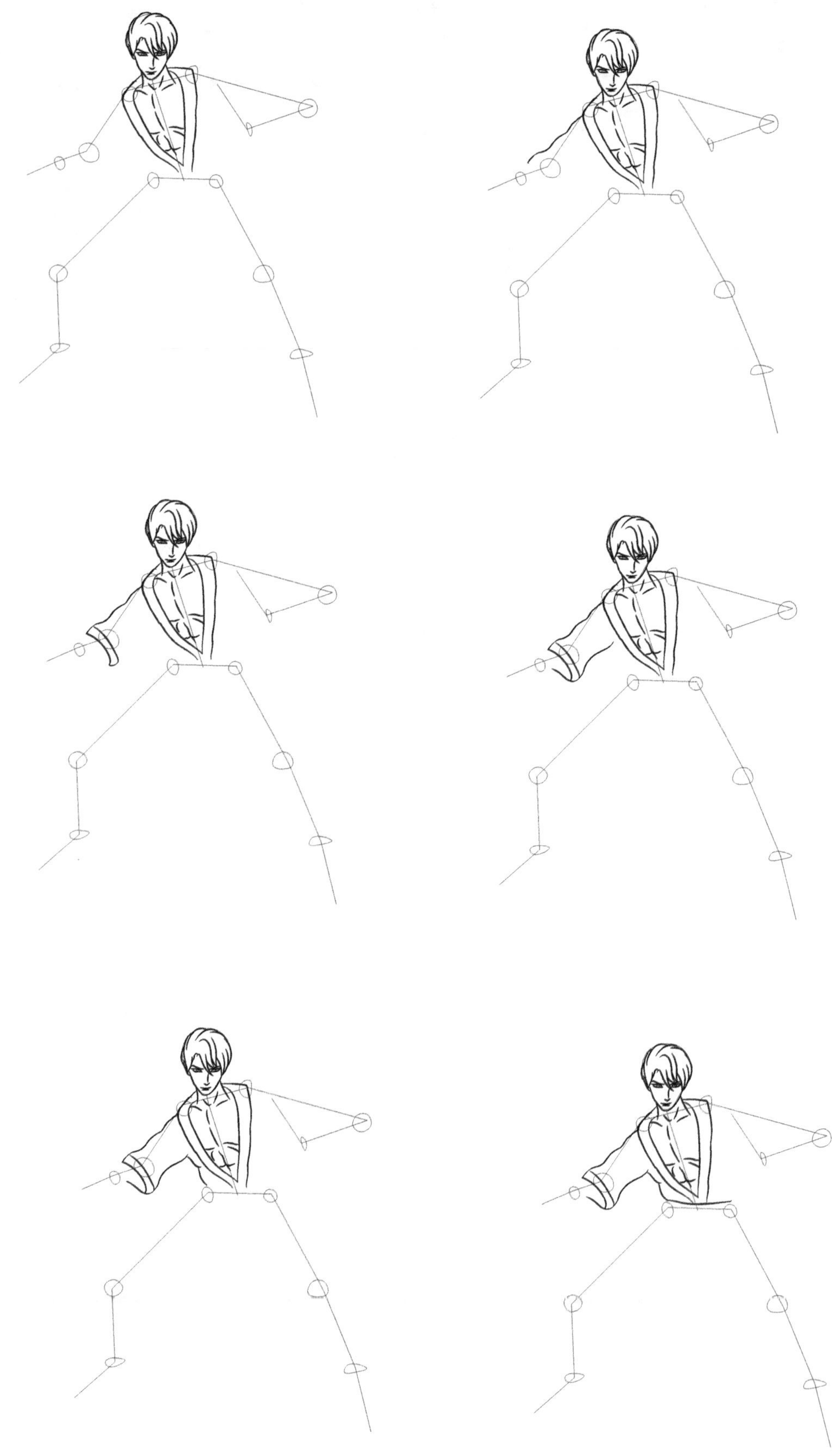

A B C D E F G H
1
2
3
4
5
6
7
8
9
10
11
12

18. Placing ellipses where you character has joints can often help when developing a plan for your character.

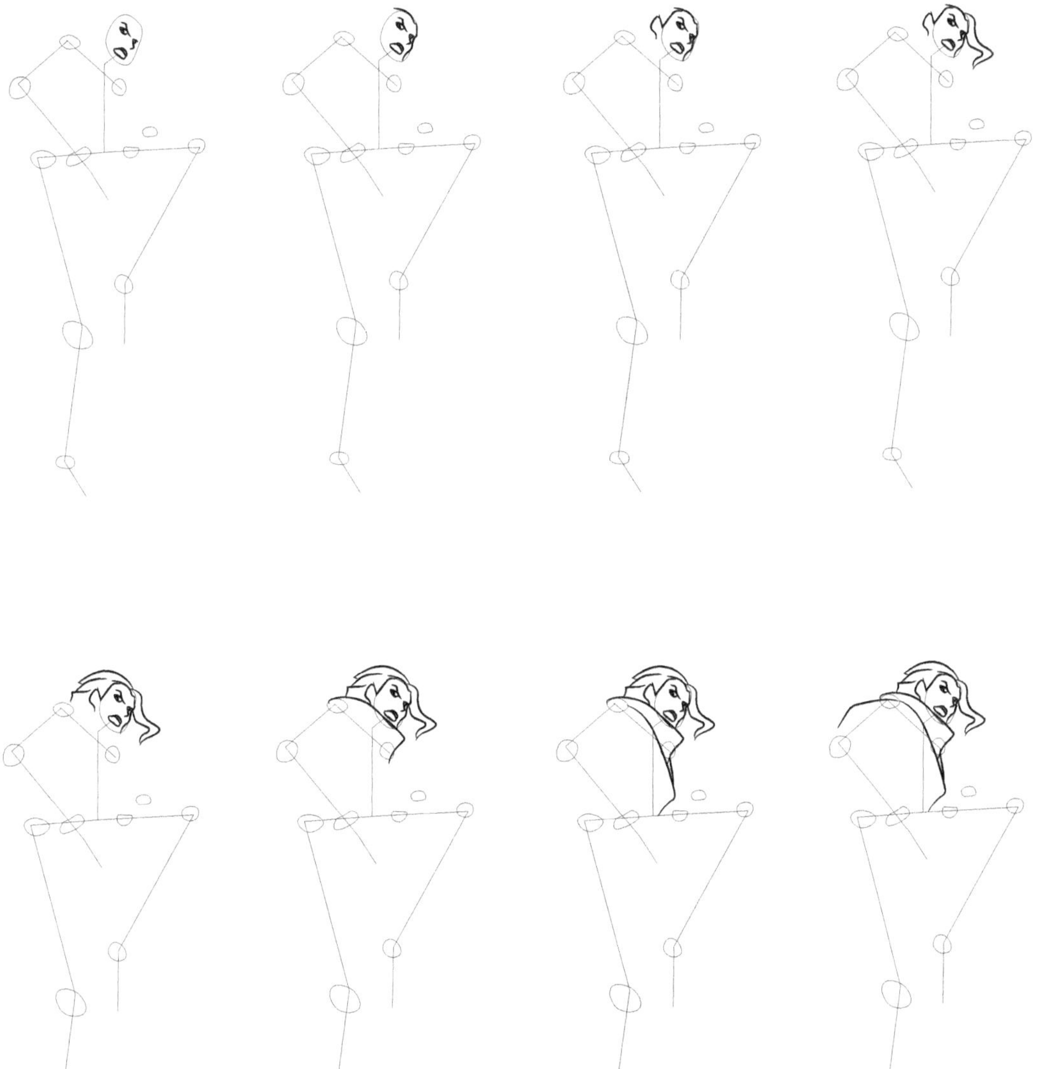

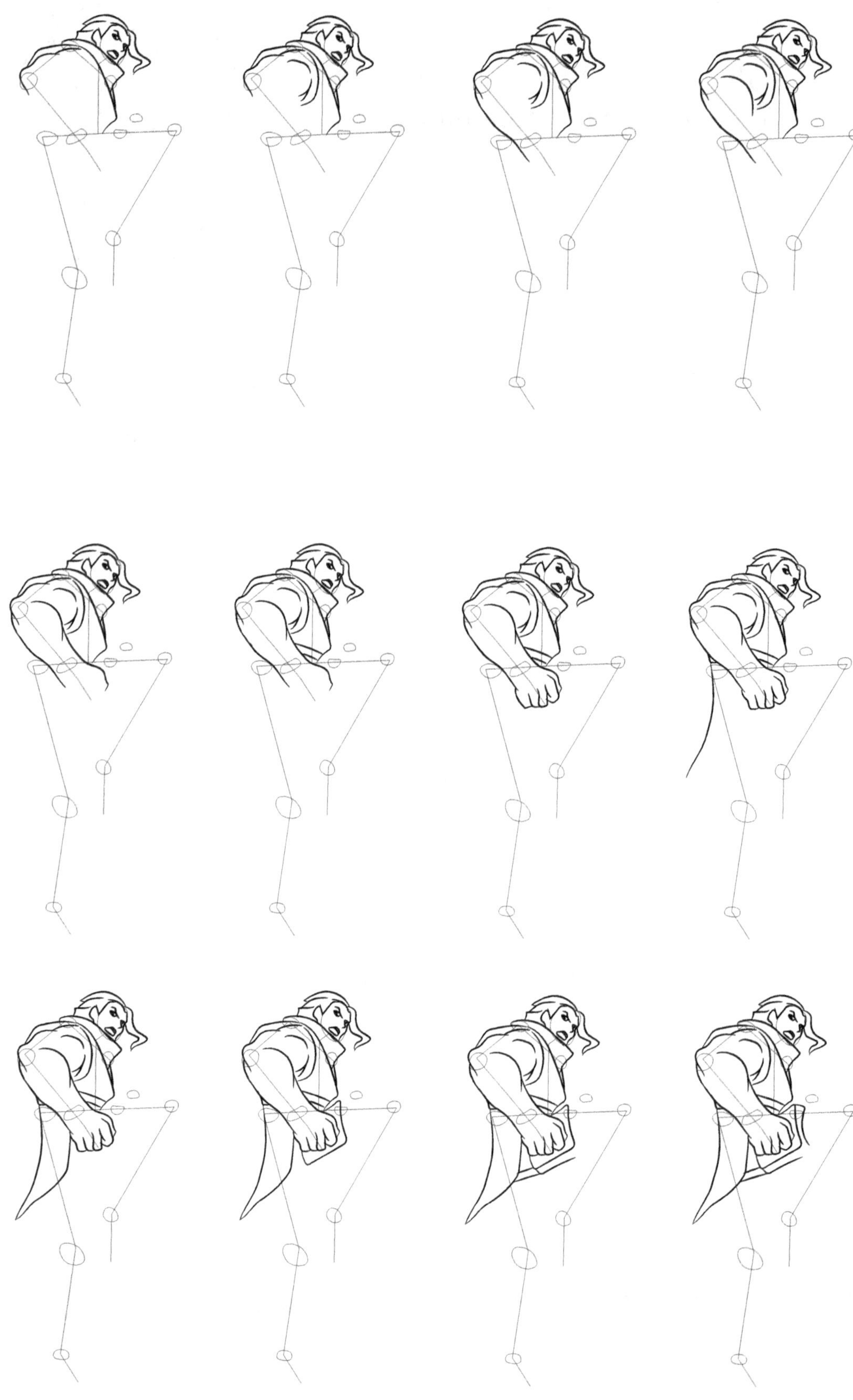

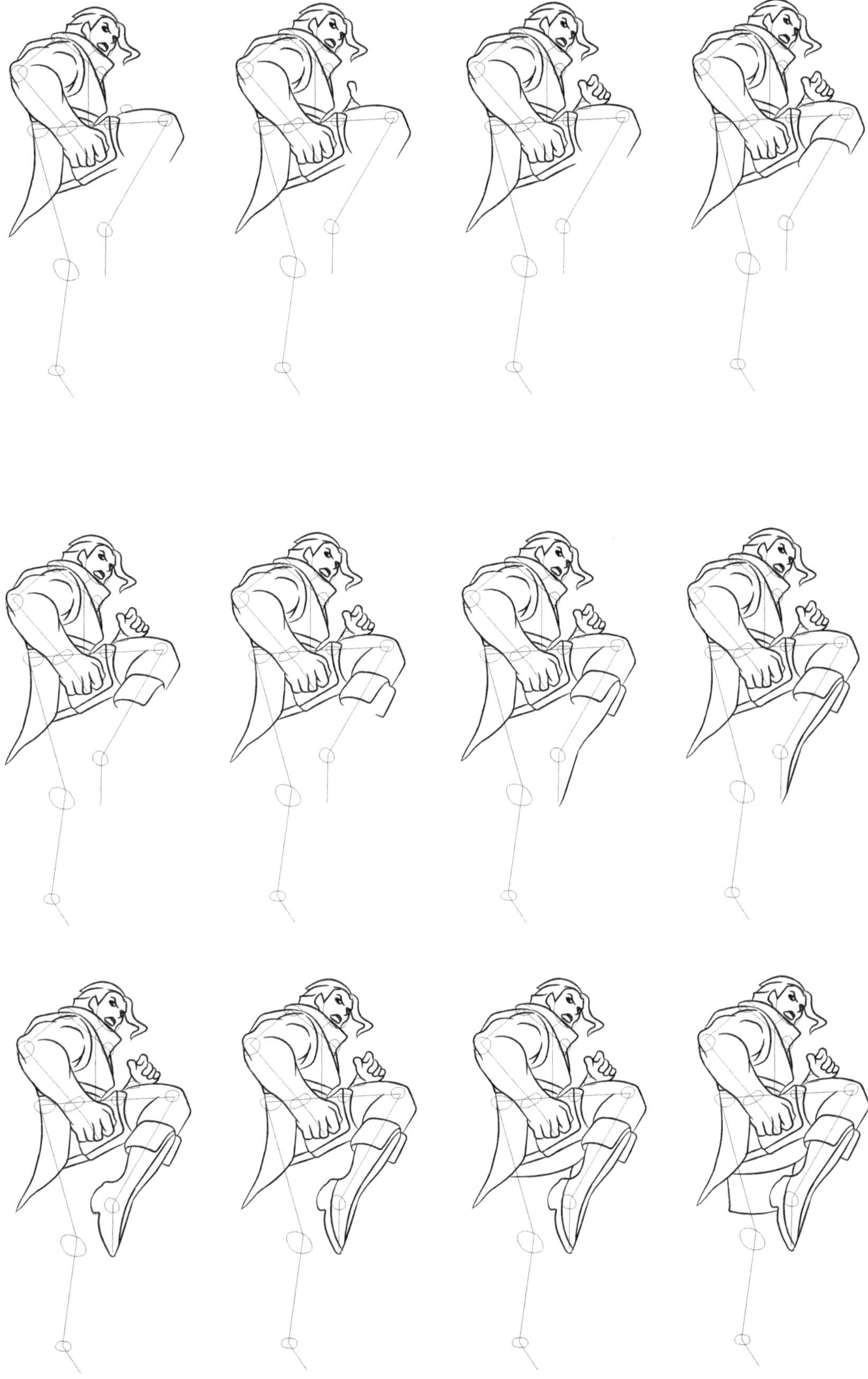

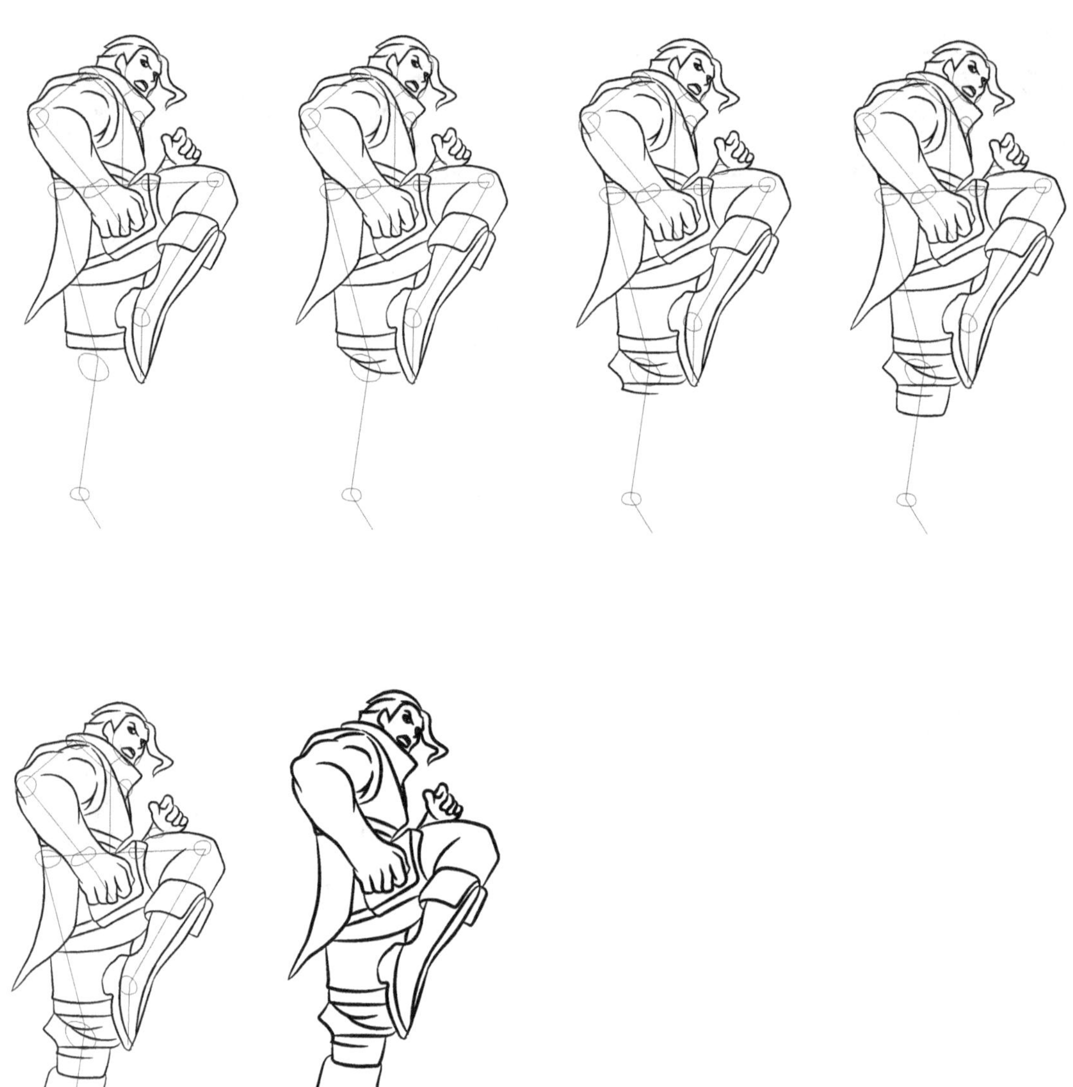

19. For larger projects focus on one step at a time. People have walked thousands of miles by taking one step at a time.

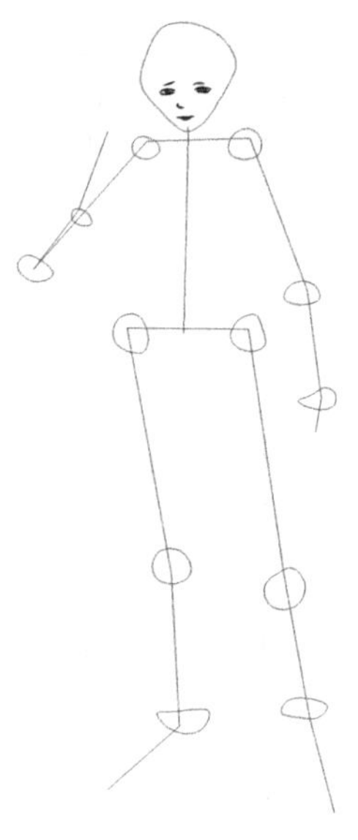
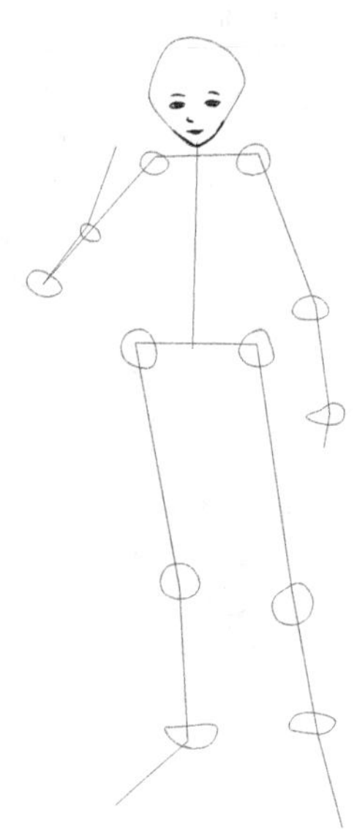
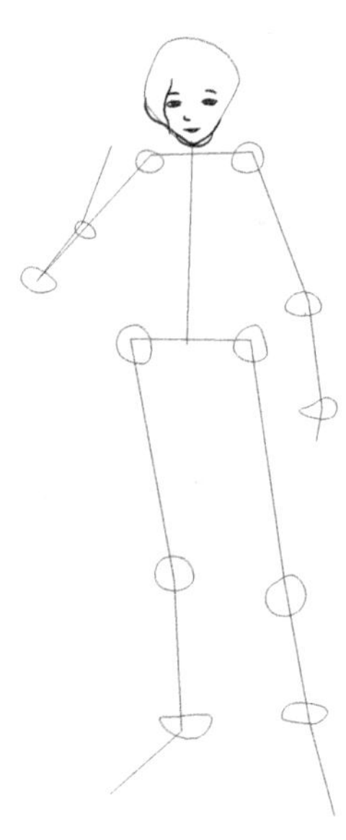

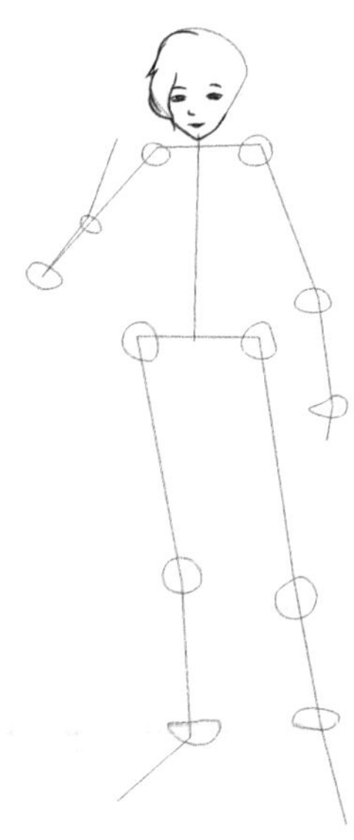
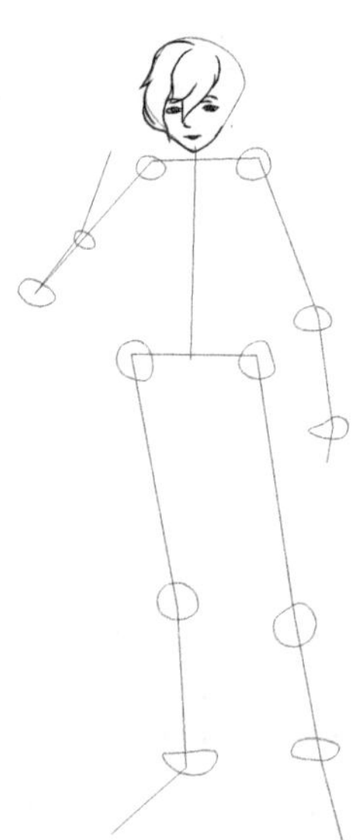
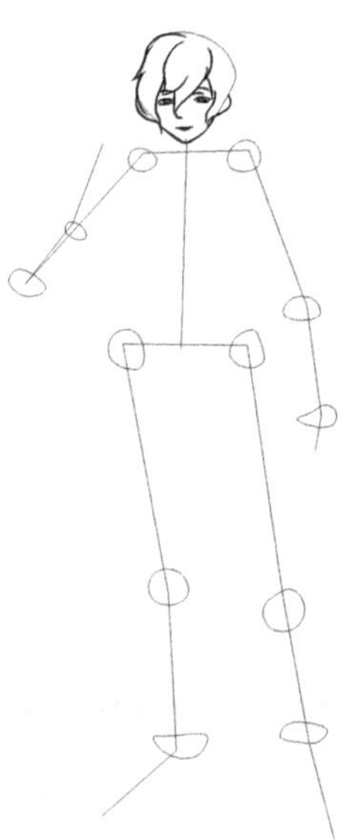

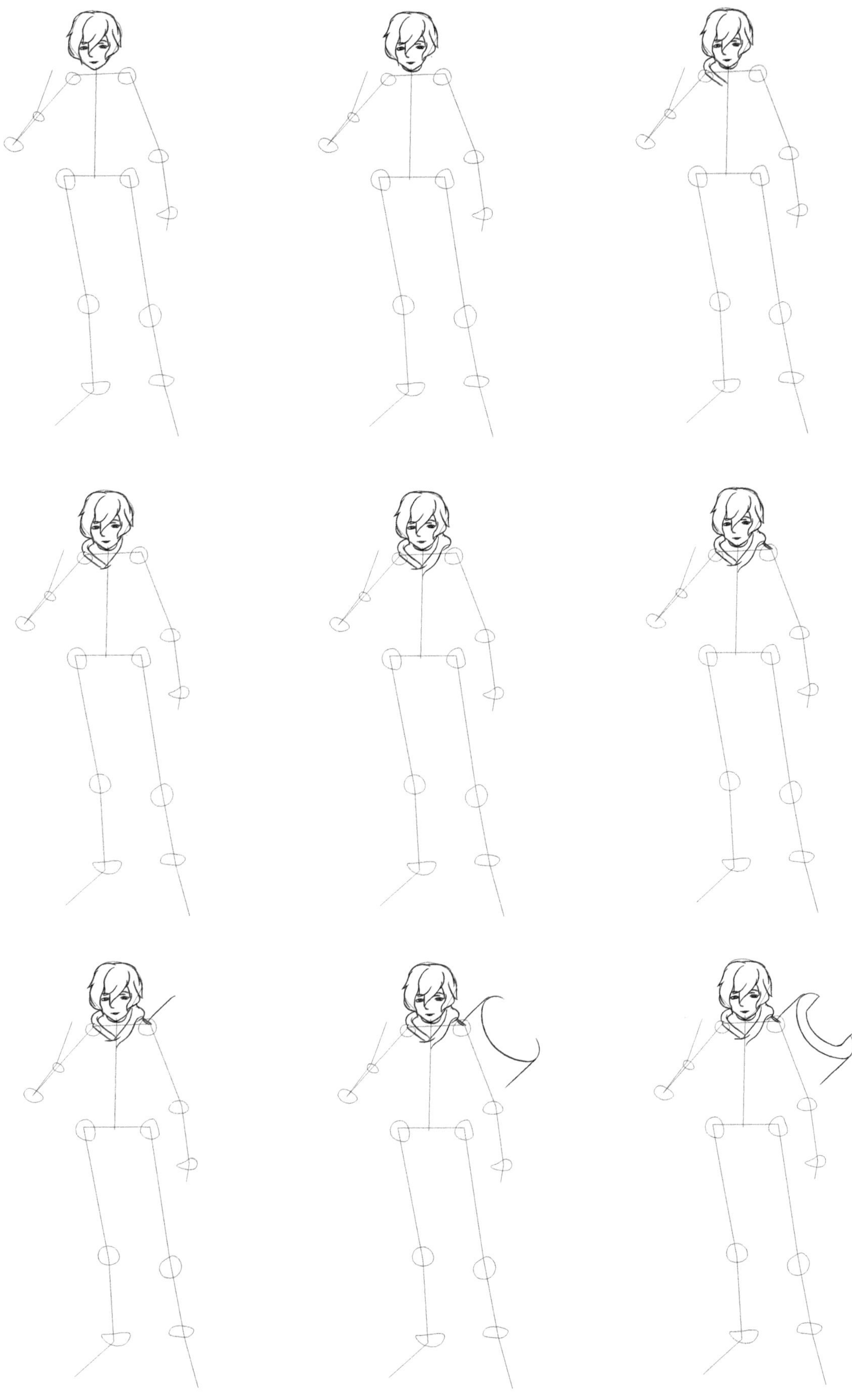

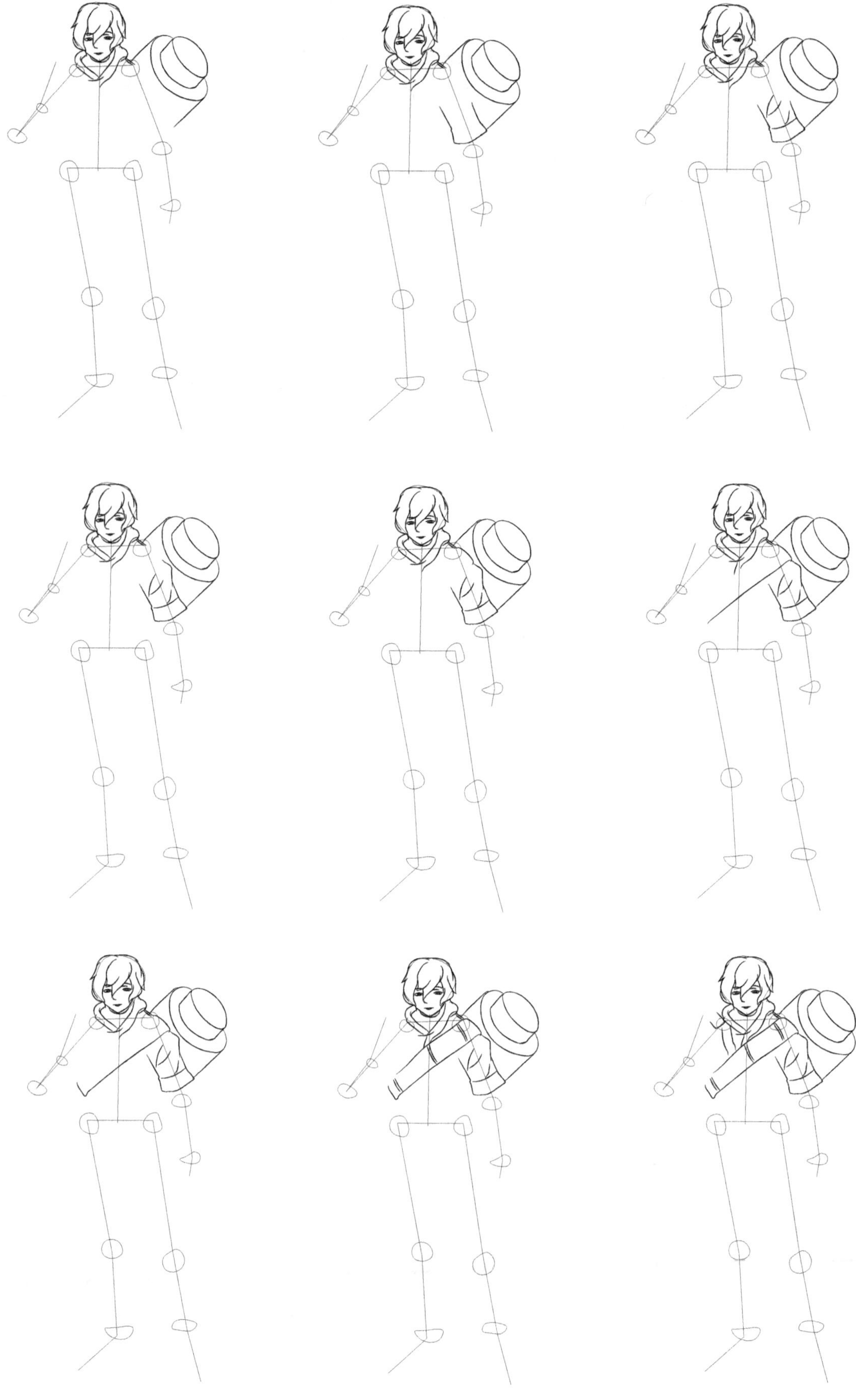

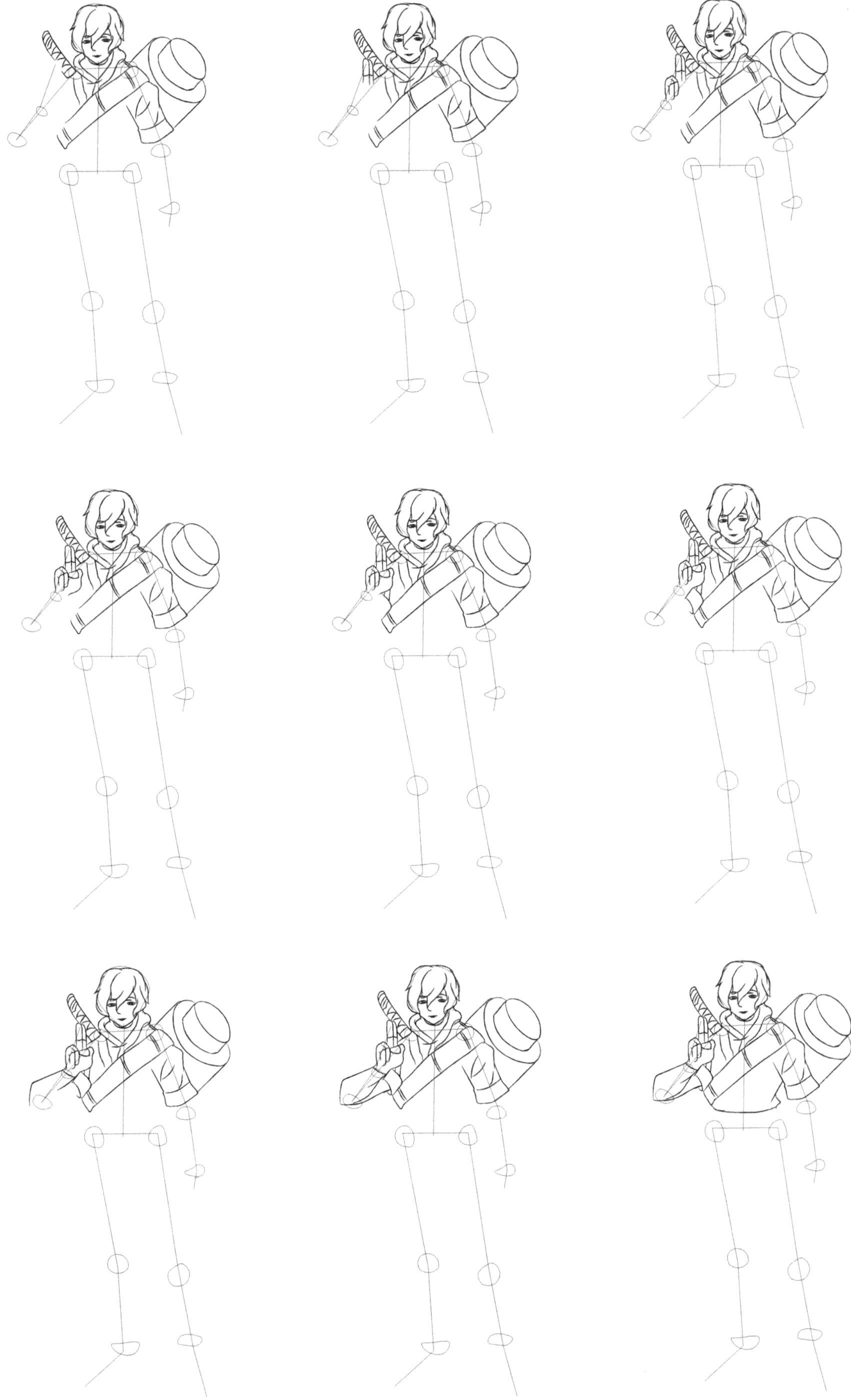

20. Characters who adjust their sleeves to
expose their wrists are suggesting
non-verbally that they are willing and able to
engage in physical activity.

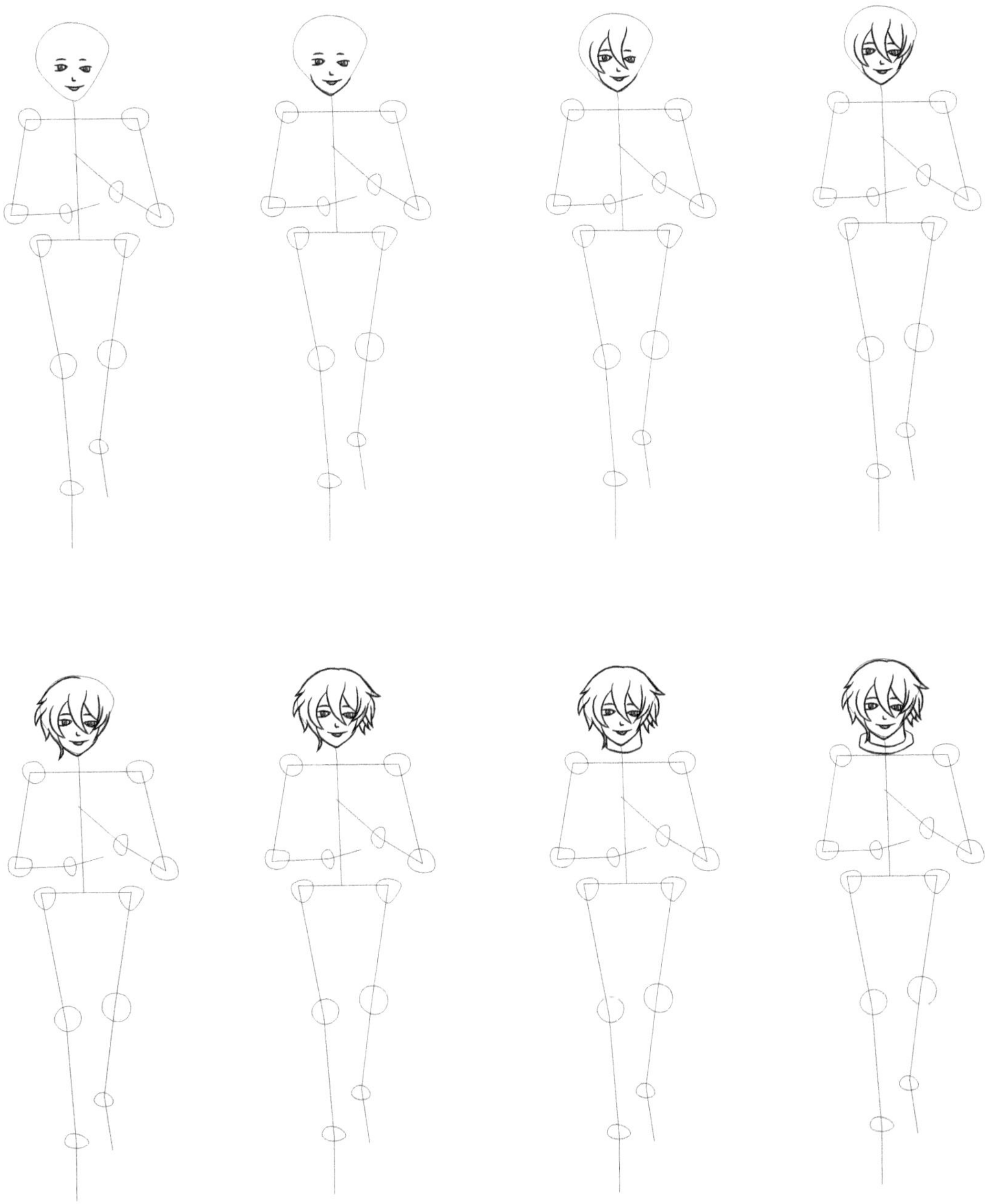

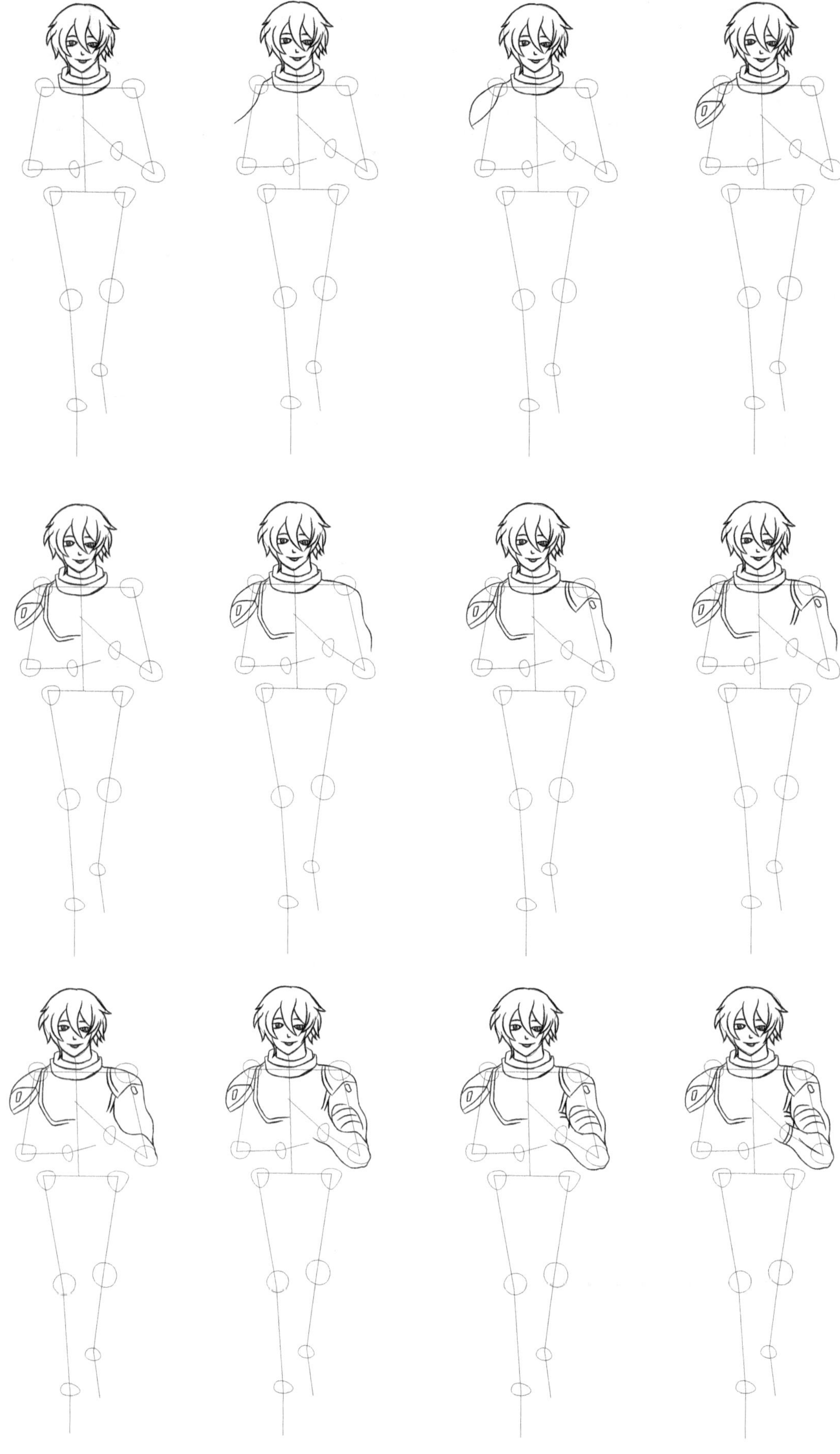

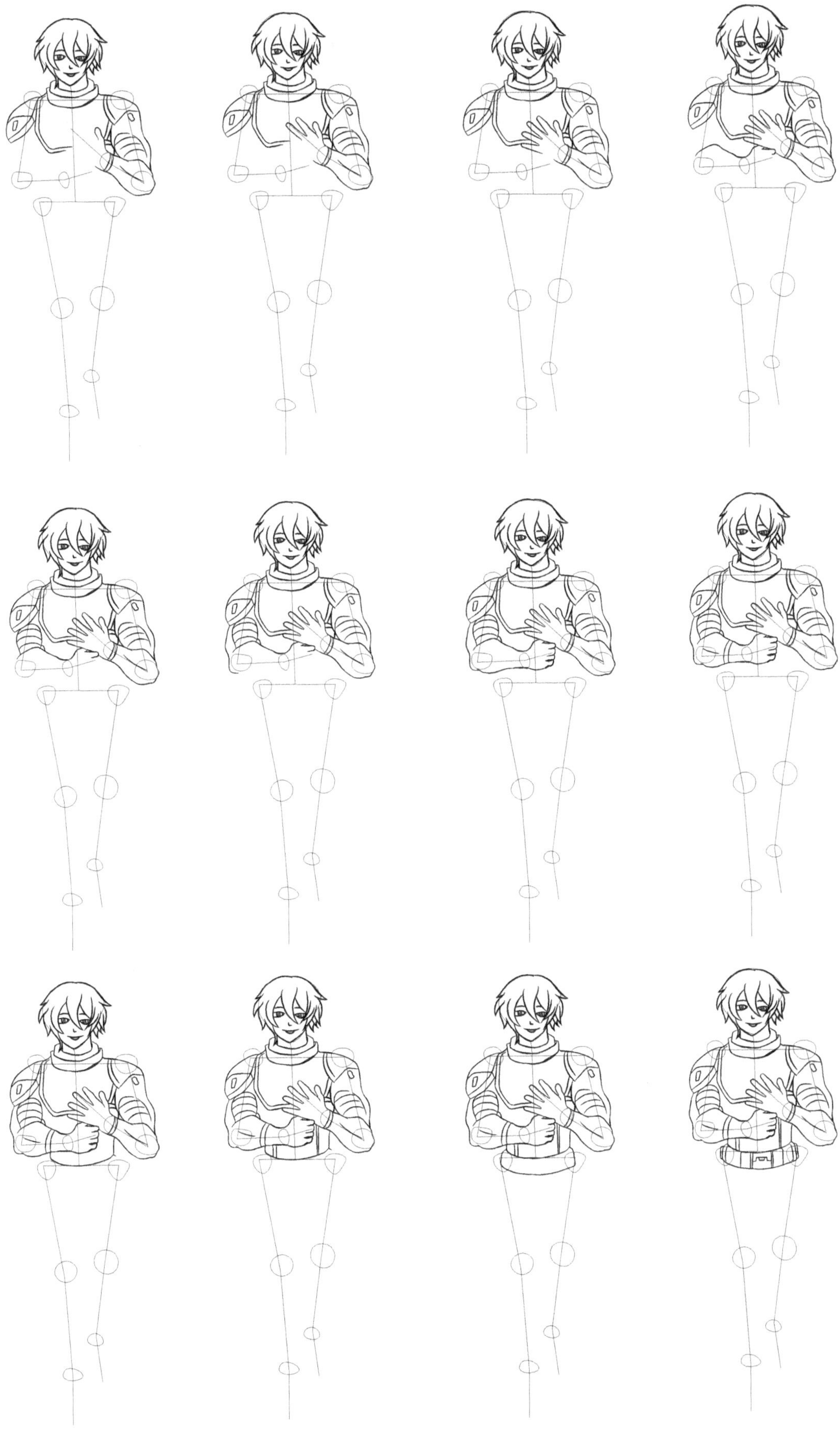

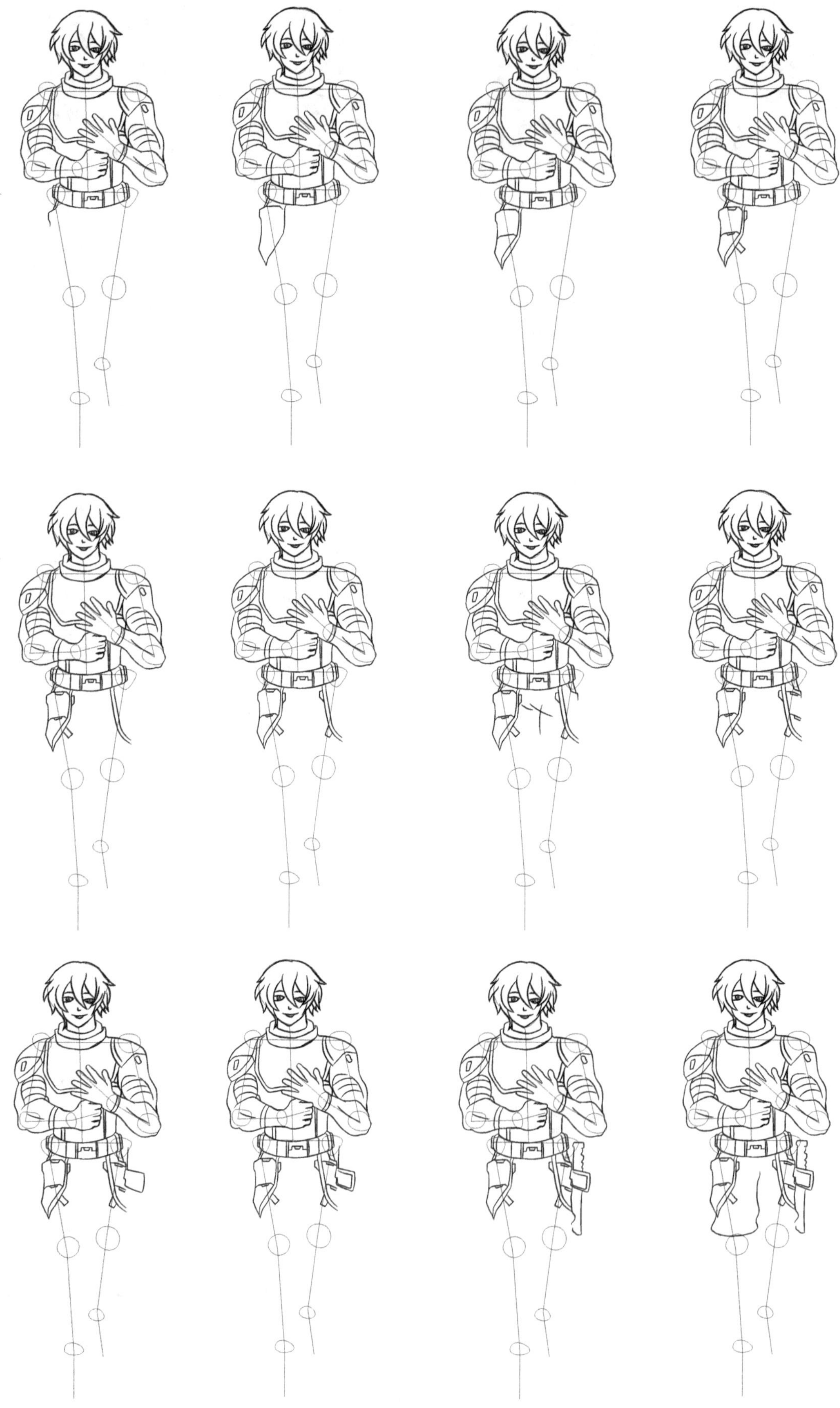

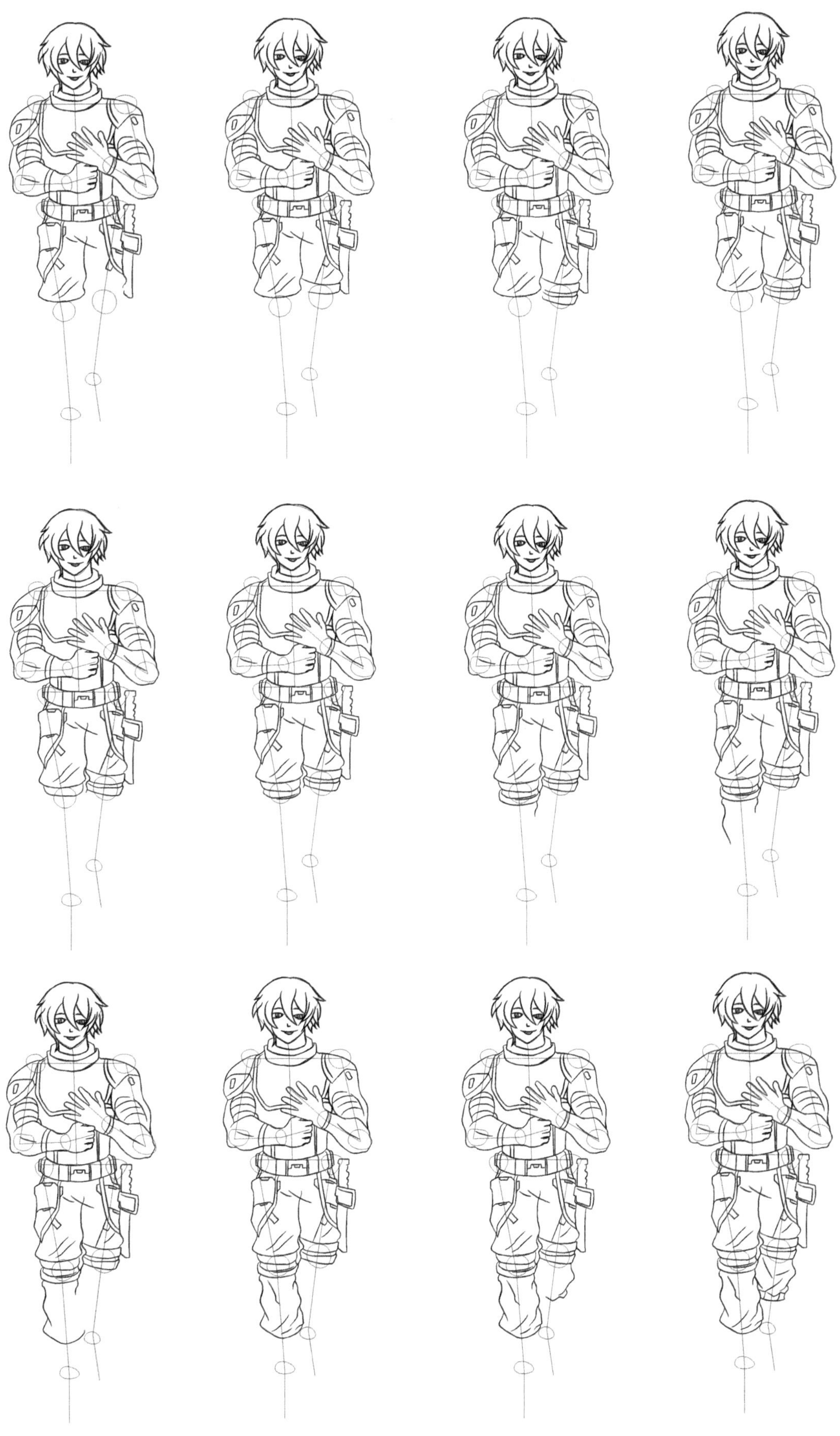

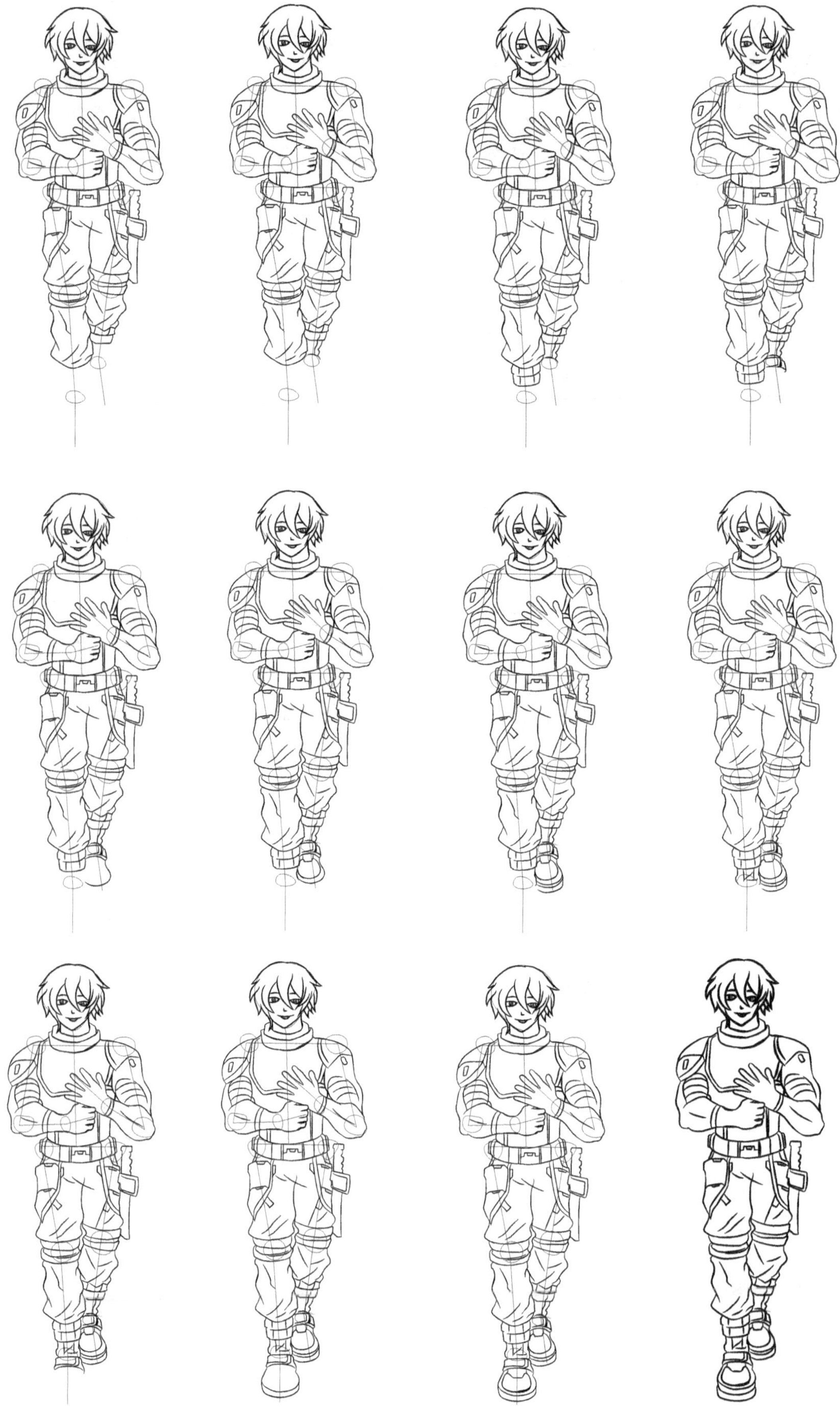

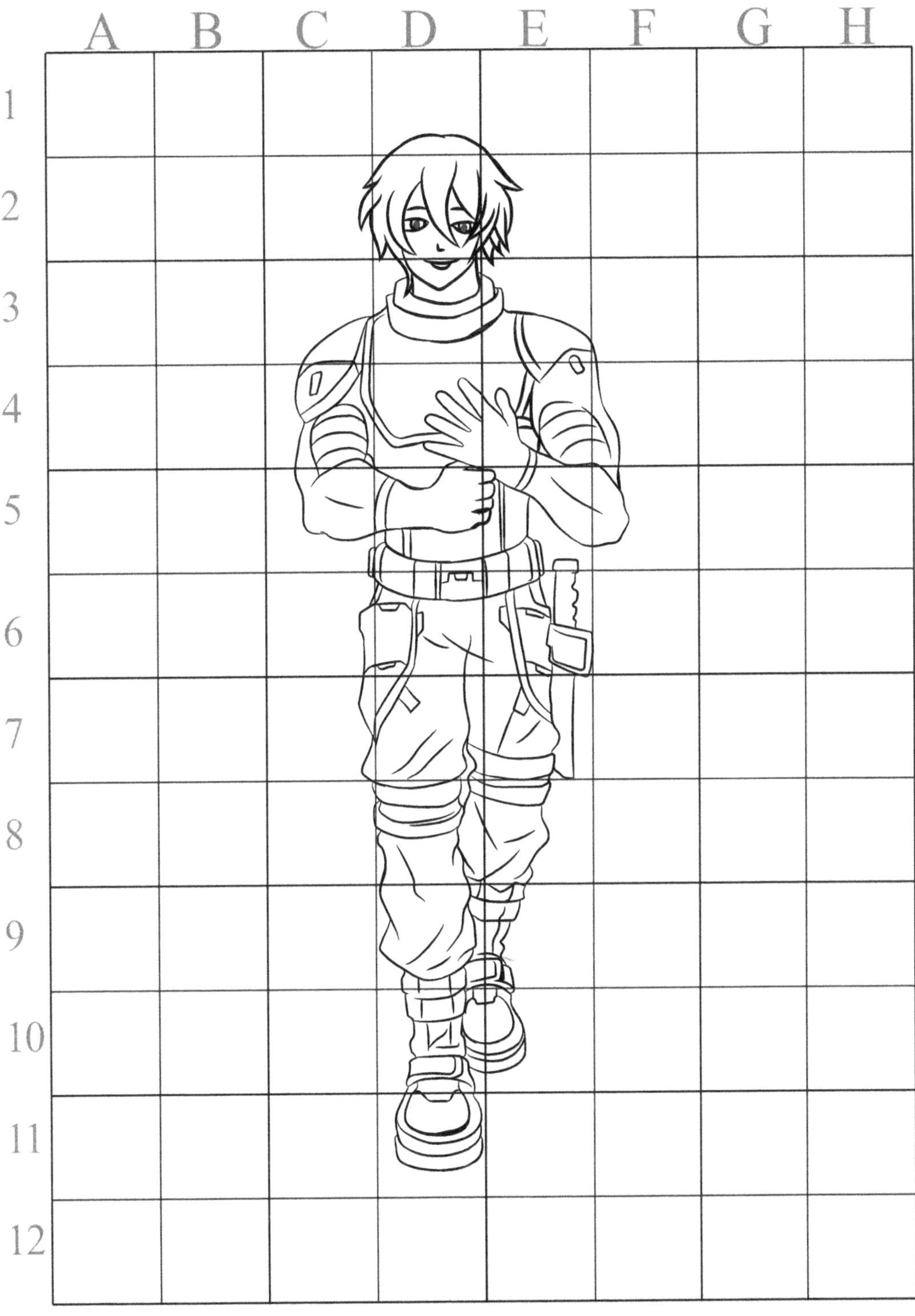

A B C D E F G H
1
2
3
4
5
6
7
8
9
10
11
12